T0353699

Independent

The Journey of a Sigma Male

Michael Zareski

BALBOA.PRESS

A DIVISION OF HAY HOUSE

Balboa Press books may be ordered through booksellers or by contacting:

Balboa Press
A Division of Hay House
1663 Liberty Drive
Bloomington, IN 47403
www.balboapress.com
844-682-1282

Because of the dynamic nature of the Internet, any web addresses or links contained in this book may have changed since publication and may no longer be valid. The views expressed in this work are solely those of the author and do not necessarily reflect the views of the publisher, and the publisher hereby disclaims any responsibility for them.

The author of this book does not dispense medical advice or prescribe the use of any technique as a form of treatment for physical, emotional, or medical problems without the advice of a physician, either directly or indirectly. The intent of the author is only to offer information of a general nature to help you in your quest for emotional and spiritual well-being. In the event you use any of the information in this book for yourself, which is your constitutional right, the author and the publisher assume no responsibility for your actions.

Any people depicted in stock imagery provided by Getty Images are models, and such images are being used for illustrative purposes only.
Certain stock imagery © Getty Images.

Print information available on the last page.

ISBN: 979-8-7652-5860-6 (sc)
ISBN: 979-8-7652-5859-0 (e)

Library of Congress Control Number: 2024926677

Balboa Press rev. date: 12/27/2024

Introduction

In the fall of 1988, while having a snooze on the couch at home in Dartmouth, I had a vivid dream that I would now call a premonition of events to come. In this dream I could see myself climbing a tall ladder and as I stretched to reach for the top rung, I fell all the way to the bottom landing not on the ground but in an extensive labyrinth of underground tunnels and passageways. In the tunnels I was met by an older, wiser oriental person who was waiting for me to lead me through the maze.

In this dream the ladder scene would represent my climbing to the top of my conscious outward journey in material life as represented by my career, accomplishments, and status in the community. The underground labyrinth would represent a journey into the deep inner subconscious realms and the older, wiser oriental person would be a guide taking me through those realms. In my quest to know myself, it was necessary to go within to gain an understanding of the mysteries of life and this was now the path that lay ahead of me. I did not know at the time of the dream what lay ahead but intuitively I knew to take things one step at a time following my intuition and internal guidance... that is my journey.

In June 1990, the whispered controversy surrounding the Buchanan government patronage practices reached a crescendo when in my position as the former Deputy Minister of the Government Services Department, I leveled widespread corruption charges that reached directly into the Premier's office.

In the weeks following the explosive allegations I went on to release a steady flow of other minor and major scandals, revelations and allegations that served to confirm the general truth that Nova Scotia politics is a patronage cesspool.

"Honest John" a moniker that Buchanan proudly cultivated as Premier of the Progressive Conservative Party of Nova Scotia, vehemently denied my testimony that he accepted kickbacks and personally interfered with government spending decisions by directing work to friends. Yet two months later, he abruptly resigned in the middle of an RCMP criminal investigation to accept a Senate appointment offered by his close friend and confident Prime Minister Brian Mulroney, Leader of the Conservative Party of Canada.

For months prior to this politically explosive appearance before the legislature's Public Accounts Committee, members of the Buchanan government had been quietly spreading stories among my friends, former colleagues, and members of the media: about my mental state, religious beliefs, the circumstances of my divorce, and about how and why I had left my job as the Deputy Minister of Government Services.

The reason given for the invitation to attend Public Accounts as a witness was allegedly to discuss government leases. However, as the hearing went on, it became abundantly clear that the government members on the committee had an alternative agenda. Their line of questioning was obviously intended to publicly discredit me and my reputation. The whisper campaign of the last few months had been elevated into the public domain.

About ten years ago several banker boxes full of documents and correspondence were taken out of storage with the goal of writing a book based on my experiences with the Nova Scotia political system. The only problem was that my state of mind was not sufficiently detached from those life-changing events and the more I wrote the angrier I became. The documentation and my memories on what had happened was too upsetting to deal with so I resolved to let sleeping dogs lie. The project was abandoned and boxes full of documents were destroyed in a backyard bonfire. At that time the act of cleansing by fire those upsetting and negative emotions allowed me to get on with my life, it did not however remove the desire to eventually tell my side of the story.

I know now that the book had to be written from a state of peace and acceptance based on my recollection and feelings of what had transpired during my time in government and the resultant consequences of the decision to speak the truth and shed light on these matters.

This book is about my journey as an independent minded individual who has throughout life trusted my intuition and inspiration in all that I do, especially in my stand for the truth against corruption in spite of how the world, my employer, my family, my friends, and colleagues wanted me to behave. It is about my suspicions arrived at during my time as a civil servant,that all levels of government were self-serving institutions doing the bidding of unelected authorities from whom they take direction - not the people. A fact that subsequent investigations corroborated to be the case.

Our birthrights as sovereign free peoples have been stolen from us through deceit and subterfuge to exploit the many by the few. It is a book of awakening to a litany of lies passed on as truth by these nefarious global controllers who see themselves as the arbitrators of the information age through which they have managed and directed the narrative for far too long.

These experiences and findings are brought to your attention to let you know and understand that something is going on. Many have uncovered the truth and figured out how to use the rules of the game to our advantage - this can be accomplished by you as well. Collectively we can take back control of our lives and we are there to help one another do this.

My choice to stand for the truth against corruption was passing a test in a way. Was I going to stand for the light? Was I going to stand for love? Was I going to stand for truth and wisdom in spite of what's around me or what the world wants me to do? This was in fact a series of tests that I have faced since I was young and through this journey, I know that always standing up for spirituality, always standing up for the light, for the truth no matter how the world wanted me to behave is the only way.

The book provides hope and a way forward for all of us to transition from the final stages of the Piscean Age into the Age of Aquarius, the Golden Age of peace, truth, and enlightenment where self-determination and growth is the norm, not the exception.

CHAPTER 1

The Early Days

Six months after graduation from the Technical University of Nova Scotia in 1972 with a degree in civil engineering, I was hired as a young engineer in the Department of Public Works. It was an opportunity that came out of left field. My previous summer jobs were with the Department of Highways doing survey work and considering that patronage paid a role through family connections with Hon. Garnet Brown the Minister of Highways under the Liberal government in having me hired it came as a surprise to me and to my classmates that after graduation a much-coveted position as an engineer-in-training with the highways department did not materialize. As a consolation, the surveyor position held the previous summer was re-offered and accepted. The job with Public Works came about towards the end of the summer after my brother who had been working as an aide to one of the government ministers happened to mention to Don Power, the Deputy Minister of Public Works that his brother was looking for work as an engineer.

At that time my father was fighting a rare form of leukemia and although he was in remission he was not doing well. A year later the business he operated as a sole proprietor, needed help and I left the security of my government job to join him as a sales engineer for Corrosion Control Ltd., the Atlantic Canadian agent of Amercoat of Canada who manufactured protective coatings, grouts, and membranes for marine and heavy industrial applications to protect steel and concrete from corrosion and deterioration. My father had built up the business with several solid accounts that needed support and due to his illness, it was clearly too much for him to handle alone. With the cancer quickly spreading the health of this gregarious larger-than-life dynamic individual quickly deteriorated, and in June of 1974 he lost his battle leaving behind my mother and a family of fourteen children of which I was the oldest boy.

In taking over the reins of the business, it quickly became apparent how financially strapped the company was and as well how large business operates, especially in Atlantic Canada. To win contracts, the manufacturer would discount the bid by offering a discount and then upon winning the contract take the discount offered from my commission. Under the circumstances, it was almost impossible to cover expenses and I was operating at best on a break-even basis. This was not sustainable, and a program of consolidation was necessary including the collection of outstanding payments and negotiated settlement with the bank and creditors leading to the winding down of the company.

As one door closes, another door opens, and this door was an opportunity to return to Public Works. On a business trip to Cape Breton, I bumped into Don Power at the Halifax Airport, and he mentioned that the department would be starting the design and construction of the Nova Scotia Rehabilitation Centre and asked if I would consider coming back to work on the project. There was no hesitation, and the offer was accepted immediately.

The Rehab Centre was certainly a challenging project. It involved a new concept in delivering projects known as construction management. Traditionally, an architect and his team would complete the design drawings and specifications which would be publicly tendered. Upon the receipt and evaluation of the bids received the project would be awarded to the lowest bidder that met all the requirements and the general contractor would carry out the work for a fixed lump sum price using his own forces and designated sub-contractors and suppliers.

In this new concept the design and construction were phased with the advantage of compressing the time frame between the start of design and completion of construction. The initial phase of the work which included site excavation, footings, foundations, and structure was designed and awarded to trade contractors who were coordinated by a an independently selected Construction Manager who also coordinated the supply of all common general condition items needed by these companies. As Phase 1 was progressing the design of the subsequent phases were being finalized for tender and award.

The task of developing the contract documents to establish in clear and concise terms the roles, relationship and responsibilities between the various parties including the government, the construction manager, the various trade contractors, and the designers was assigned to me. This was done in the days of manual typewriters and gestetner copiers. After many long hours literally cutting and pasting documents at home on evenings and weekends and returning the latest draft for retyping, the final documents was completed. The document subsequently formed the basis of the construction management standard form contract documents used by the Nova Scotia and Canadian Construction Associations.

To make things more challenging there was a project strike by the plumber's union which delayed construction progress. Notwithstanding, the government of the day under Gerald Reagan set the 25th of June 1977 as the official opening date and that was not negotiable. The pressure was on, a few days before the opening ceremony there was still lots of work to do. While preparations for the opening were underway, the more important planning to make ready for the occupancy of the building by staff and patients was the primary focus. During an orientation tour for the building medical staff, a nurse accosted me in the elevator saying, "Mr. Zareski you can't honestly believe that this building will be ready to move patients in next week."

On the day of the opening, as speeches were being given outside, the cleaning crews were working their way down through the building doing final touch-ups. When the top floor was finished the okay was given for the tour to start with the entourage entering an area made ready just in the nick of time. Both the official opening and subsequent occupancy were completed without a hitch and the building was turned over to the staff and patients on schedule.

A hospital accreditation team made up of rehabilitation health care officials from across Canada stated in their report that the Nova Scotia Rehabilitation Hospital was the finest example of a rehabilitation hospital that they have seen to date.

Following the successful completion of the project, my career with Public Works was on an upward trajectory going on to become the Director of Construction for Nova Scotia Department of Public Works responsible for the supervision and management of all aspects of the design and construction contracted through private sector architects, engineers, and contractors.

At this time, I was living in Dartmouth and starting a family. One Saturday, my wife attended a Psychic Fair held at a local community recreation facility. On returning home she shared the cassette tape of her reading from the clairvoyant which was more about me than her. My interest was piqued and the next afternoon I attended for myself hoping to get my own session. Arriving at the booth, there were a half dozen people waiting and a longer sign-in list. As I was about to leave the reader had just finished her last session and came out, picked up the list and called out the next name. Getting no response, she looked at me and invited me to fill the slot for the no show.

My reading started with the following lines that she was tapping into from 'my spirit guides'. "Firm of face, firm of feet, firm of goals and all he'll meet." During the session she informed me that I was a "Starseed", a term that I was not familiar with, and she suggested that I read more about it and recommended books like by "The Star People" by Brad and Francie Steiger, and "Chariots of the Gods" by Erich Von Daniken.

My foot was now on the path and my spiritual journey was rekindled from my days at university when I mused about the nature of God and reality. The age-old questions have never left me, who am I, why am I here, what is my purpose. Believing that there is more to life than what is perceived through the five senses, the journey for truth began. This was a solitary journey for me as the topics I was interested in were not openly discussed in a strict Roman Catholic upbringing where you were taught to honor your father and mother and that the priest, politician and doctor were infallible. The trouble was, the older I got the more apparent it became that the paradigm was falling apart. As a young altar boy, I could not accept the necessity of confession through a priest who would intercede with God on my behalf…if I needed to speak to God, I could do so on my own.

I was interested in the integration of rationality and spirituality through the wisdom that can be gleaned from the knowledge of the physical and the metaphysical world. Through my training as an engineer, I supplemented engineering education with electives in the humanities. My feeling was that engineers were too rational and too logical, too analytical. It is important to develop the feeling aspects of my personality. My engineering training and career path was based on physical observation, leading to logical outcomes. I was constantly trying to balance that with honing intuitive skills. Shakespeare's line from Hamlet, "There are more things in heaven and earth, Horatio, than are dreamt of in your philosophy." was often recalled when something out of the ordinary or unexpected occurred, it is confirmation that there was much more to life than what is perceived through the five senses. The age-old maxim "Know Thyself" is the goal like the proverbial carrot on the end of the stick that keeps me searching.

Years later at a Christmas get together, I was having an engaging conversation with a new neighbour on metaphysical topics. He suggested I might be interested in learning more through an organization called the Ancient Mystical Order Rosae Crucis also known by the acronym AMORC whose members are commonly referred to as a Rosicrucian and a few days later dropped off an application form. Upon being accepted a more focused metaphysical study began.

AMORC is a worldwide fraternity of men and women from all walks of life who study mysticism, science and the arts in order to understand man's relationship with the Divine. Some of the world's greatest thinkers were Rosicrucians such as Benjamin Franklin, Francis Bacon, Socrates and Plato. Through the Order, the esoteric wisdom of the universe is passed down from ancient times with the goal of gaining insight into the ultimate reality, independent of the apparatus of organized religious dogma and doctrine.

As Director of Construction reporting to Don Power, the Deputy Minister, I was responsible for the design and construction of several significant projects including hospitals, education facilities and museums. Mr. Power was a diligent, hard-working, and tough taskmaster who had his thumb on all aspects of the Department of Public Works...nothing was done without his blessing. Those who worked with him, including politicians, had a great deal of respect for his knowledge of government and his ability to get things done.

There were those including myself who did not always agree with his decisions; however, I was one of the few who when not seeing eye-to-eye, was not afraid to question him and would often say "Mr. Power you are not always right but you're always the boss. I will do what you ask." He seemed to appreciate that I was not a 'yes' man that I was not afraid to tell him what I thought, even though it was not necessarily what he wanted to hear. It got to a point where he would often ask my advice or there were other times when I would give him advice and he would say something to the effect that 'Zareski don't be so foolish that's a crazy idea, that will never work, forget about it.' Then some weeks later he would come back to me with the same plan of attack, and I would reply 'That's a great idea, I'll get on it right away.' never mentioning that it was my idea in the first place. Early on I learned that in order to move things in a positive direction, it was necessary to plant the seed and let it come to fruition by having the decision makers think it was their idea in the first place. That was how we worked together, and my job was to do the work to the best of my ability and make him look good in the eyes of his political masters.

There was a lot of responsibility on my plate, however, as was Power's style, he was the ultimate decision maker and did not delegate authority to anyone. This was put to the test during one of the onsite construction meetings for the Adult Vocational Training Centre in Sydney Cape Breton when several site coordination issues raised by the contractors had to be dealt with to keep the project on schedule. Rather than take the issues back to Halifax to review with Power and finalize the changes that had to be made, a process that could take several weeks, I took it upon myself to give the necessary directions to the contractors to keep the project moving. Upon returning to Halifax, I reviewed the actions taken and decisions made with Power, who was clearly upset and reprimanded me for usurping his authority. I countered firmly taking the position that if you are going to send me to represent the department that I must have the authority to do so otherwise I am nothing more than an errand boy. We came to an understanding and authority, within limits was granted.

In 1978 the Progressive Conservative party under the leadership of John Buchanan won the election and was back in power. Under the previous conservative government of G.I Smith, Buchanan had been Minister of Public Works with Don Power as his deputy. The two got along well and picked up where they left off with Buchanan as Premier and the de facto Minister of Public Works. Power ran the department answering only the Premier. The government ministers including the nominal minister of Public Works and all government members, including those in opposition knew that Power had the ear of the Premier and no one challenged him. In government circles, the names 'Power' and 'God' were synonymous.

Typically, a new government coming into power will want to put their stamp on things. Premier Buchanan was no different. The internal day-to-day operations of government were disorganized and inefficient with the civil servants in several departments, agencies, and commissions vying for status under the new regime. A government reorganization was necessary.

In 1980 the management consulting firm of Coopers and Lybrand were selected for the assignment. When Coopers and Lybrand looked into the delivery of common services, for weeks they interviewed all employees of several service delivery departments in all job classifications. The consulting team were very thorough and professional, leaving no stone unturned. They were interested in what we did, who we reported to, what processes and procedures we followed, how our work was documented, what accountability we had, and all other such standard fact-finding information. Through the exercise it was found for example that a long serving employee was gathering, recording, and filing certain documents for years that no one ever used or consulted. Coopers and Lybrand teams were carrying out similar reviews in other departments and agencies.

The culmination of this effort came in late summer of 1980 at a meeting of senior management of the department and from selected other agencies. Don Power introduced the Cooper and Lybrand management team who then outlined the organizational structure, role and responsibility of the new Department of Government Services recently adopted by the Premier and cabinet. Government Services was essentially the former Public Works Department with additional divisions related to the delivery of common services that were here-to-fore being carried out by other departments, boards, and agencies.

The approved structure included four main operating divisions; Construction and Accommodations, System and Computer Services, Information Services and, Finance and Administration, with each run by an Executive Director reporting to the Deputy Minister with directors, managers, and staff to round out each division. At the end of the meeting, Don Power indicated that the twenty or so senior management positions identified on the organizational chart would be open to internal competition followed by external advertisement, except for the Executive Director of Construction and Accommodations which is set aside for Zareski.

This announcement took me by surprise and put me in a difficult position, as a thirty-year-old, it was now my responsibility to conduct interviews and recommend appointments of director level positions from among senior engineering colleagues many of whom were old enough to be my father. It was going to be difficult to get their trust and respect. After all my professional experience of less than ten years paled in comparison to most of theirs. Ultimately it ended up business as usual - the former Public Works management team were slotted into their former roles and in a very short time, our workload expanded significantly.

The division's primary responsibilities included the design, construction, renovation, alteration and maintenance of all provincial government buildings and the provision of office accommodation to government departments and agencies.

These were the early years of the Buchanan mandate, and the Premier used Don Power and Government Services to establish his legacy by embarking upon a major capital construction program including a new Art Gallery, Nautical Institute, Maritime Museum, Highway Maintenance Facility, and Ambulatory Care & Oncology Center, the department was mandated to take over school and hospital construction from the various school and hospital boards across the province. After all, if taxpayers were funding the projects, Buchanan would get recognition with his name engraved on cornerstones from one end of the province to the other.

It was Power's practice to visit the job sites on Sunday afternoons and meet with me on Monday mornings to review issues to be dealt with. One Sunday evening he called me at home very upset. Evidently, the security guard at a construction project outside of the city would not let him enter. Power had introduced himself as the Deputy Minister and the guard responded 'I don't care if you are God himself, you are not getting in.'

When Power is upset, his tendency was to curse and swear, and with the choice unfiltered profanities flinging across his lips I knew his buttons were pushed. To calm him down, I told him I would be in his office the first thing in the morning to deal with it. As a strategy, upon entering his office and before he opened his mouth, I started cursing before he did and asked if he got the guard's name so that I could get the 'bastard' fired. Power was taken back because I normally wouldn't say 'shit' if I had a mouth full of it. He completely revered his position saying, 'Don't be so hasty, he was just doing his job.' That afternoon instructions were given to allow Power to enter the job site after hours whenever he wished and the matter was resolved.

To manage the hospital expansion program the Hospital Construction Management Committee consisting of the Deputy Ministers of Health, Management Board, Finance and Government Services was established. I, along with several other senior civil servants were invitees to the meetings and provided the support and follow up to the Deputies. Mr. Power, not being comfortable in such venues, preferring smaller more intimate meetings which he could control. At this meeting he had me sit at his left hand and would often turn to me saying 'Michael, please explain...' or after he made a statement that was somewhat incoherent, I would find myself saying, 'What Mr. Power means to say is this...' I soon became the go to person with respect to the implementation of the hospital design and construction activities around the province and would be sent to deal with hospital boards and building committees who were at times disgruntled with new delivery method that usurped their previous authority.

On one occasion I received a call from Dr. Mickey MacDonald the Administrator of the Victoria General Hospital asking if I could stop by later that afternoon to meet with a couple of doctors to go over the plans for the new Ambulatory Care & Oncology Center at the VG. When I arrived, the boardroom was packed with standing room only. The doctors had no issues with the functional layout of the facility, they were concerned with the size of their offices. The VG, a teaching hospital affiliated with the Dalhousie Medical School was required to provide the Full-Time Equivalent (FTE) doctors with office space. The doctors wanted not only to carry out their teaching responsibilities but also run their private practices from the new building were looking for more space. To resolve the impasse, I told the meeting that arrangements would be made to change the design to accommodate the additional demands and that the doctors would have to raise the funds from their own pocket at a cost in the range of two to three hundred dollars a square foot. Not another word was said, the office space allocation was now satisfactory and the building moved forward as planned.

On another occasion, I was asked to attend the board meeting of the Abeerdeen Regional Hospital where a major expansion was underway. The hospital administrator had the board worked up to a frenzy with a litany of fabricated problems and complaints with the Government Services management of the project. He clearly wanted to kick Government Services out and take over. The chair of the board gave a brief introduction and immediately opened with an attack. It was clear that he was primed by his administrator and wanted blood. I sat calmly and quietly taking notes and when he was finished, he gave me the opportunity to respond. I initially deferred and suggested the chair go around the table giving each board member the opportunity to raise any additional concerns while continuing to take notes. Once the board had their say, the concerns were addressed one-by-one in the order in which they were brought up. I then invited them for a tour of the construction site to review the progress of the work underway, which further supported my responses. In the end, the board expressed their appreciation for the fine job being done while the administrator stood sheepishly in the background. All's well that ends well and the project was completed on time and on budget.

Don Power was pleased with the effort and dedication that was shown to my work and clearly adopted me as his protégée. Power played his cards close to his chest and as much as he could confide in anyone, he confided in me. We spent a lot of time together and there was evidence of him taking things easier, delegating more, and taking more time for himself. A telltale signs that he was planning his exit strategy from the civil service was when travelling on business to the United States, we would fly to the closest city on economy class to comply with the government travel regulations and then upgrade our tickets to first class for the remainder of the journey. There was a typically a golf game or two or a ball game or hockey game on the itinerary.

On a trip to Toronto, we drove to Grand Island, New York to meet with Cannon Design, a leader in healthcare, to interview them for participation in the design development for the Veterans Hospital at the Camp Hill Medical Centre. The Cannon team had an impressive portfolio of leading-edge hospital work and were selected to spearhead the design team which was supplemented by local Halifax architectural and engineering firms. I was assigned the day-to-day coordination and management of the team to arrive at a preliminary design including a budget. The final submission package completed in early 1984 was well received by all stakeholders, and approved by the Hospital Construction Management Committee, ready for an early summer site development work package to get the project underway. This did not happen and for some reason the much-anticipated project was put on the backburners.

In September, the Premier, taking advantage of the Mulrooney win in Ottawa where the Tories took a decisive majority, called a snap election for November 6. For sure, the announcement of the hospital construction would come as an election promise, but it didn't. This was odd as Buchanan loved sod turning ceremonies especially when on the campaign trail.

Following the election, the reason for the project not moving forward became clear to me when Power announced his intention to retire and take over the project management role for the $30 million hospital complex. This was a plan kept close to the chest of both Power and the Premier and would have raised eyebrows if word got out during the election campaign that a senior civil servant was double dipping with a full pension and a lucrative non-compete consultancy arrangement.

CHAPTER 2

Awakening to Reality

The Provincial Conservative handily won the election. On the last day of November, Power called me to his office to let me know that this was his last day as Deputy Minister. He indicated that Cy Fear, a senior policy, and planning director for Government Services would be appointed Deputy Minister and upon his retirement a year or so later I would be taking over the helm. I listened intently to the plan and said to Mr. Power that I didn't plan to spend the next year teaching Cy Fear how to do my job and that I'll be moving on to find work in the private sector.

A few days later Premier Buchanan summoned me to his office. The Premier spoke highly of Mr. Power and it was obvious that the trust and respect that he had for him was without question. He then offered me the position of Deputy Minister and suggested that I work closely with Mr. Power who will be there to guide me. In other words, on Power's retirement, he would continue as de facto deputy, taking instructions from Buchanan to be passed on to me to implement.

The Premier concluded by indicating that from time to time there will be things asked of me that I may find difficult and wanted confirmation I would do them. I specifically recall saying 'Yes Premier I will do what I can.' That qualification of 'what I can' meant I will do what my ethics will allow me to do and that's how I have operated all along and planned to continue to operate in this new role. On December 7th the position was ratified by Legislative Counsel and the public announcement was made confirming my appointment as a Deputy Minister.

In the early days, there was a lot to be done and a lot to learn. Don Power and I met frequently, and he was helpful in guiding me through some of the politics involved with the role. Jerry Lawrence was the Minister of Government under Power and continued in that role. He did not get involved with the day-to-day operation of the department and his style was to roll his wheelchair into a meeting, do a couple of wheelies, tell a joke or two and then wheel out. He was Minister in name only with little or no interest in how Government Services was run. The department still belonged to Buchanan, and he had no intention of changing the status quo.

Early on in my role, the department received permission from the Management Board to advertise for a job opening in our stationary stockroom. The Premier advised Lawrence that he wanted the son of one of his constituents to be given consideration for the position. In my naivete, I thought that to mean to give the person an interview. The interview board, following the prescribed procedures of the Civil Service Commission rated and ranked the candidates and recommended the most qualified person for the job. With civil service approval the job was offered and accepted by the successful candidate - not the Premier's man. No sooner was the ink wet on the offer, than I received a call from the Minister who was irate. He had received a call from the Premier who tore a strip off him for not following through with the patronage appointment. I settled the Minister down by telling him I would call the Premier right away to resolve the matter. I called Buchanan immediately telling him that his candidate was clearly overqualified for the job and that we have something much more suitable that he could start right away. Next, a call to the hiring manager with instructions that a new role be made in her group to be filled immediately. A valuable lesson learned - patronage was alive and well in Nova Scotia and it went right to the top. Since then, there was an unwritten understanding with the Premier, the non-skilled jobs belonged to him and the technical positions requiring professional qualifications and experience would go through the proper channels.

The construction tendering policy followed by Government Services and Public Works before it, was based on the principle that the bidder with the lowest complete tendered will be awarded the job. This policy was strictly enforced by Power and now that he was gone, the government through the Department of Development wanted to make changes by giving Nova Scotia contractors an advantage.

Minister Lawrence and I were invited to a meeting with Rollie Thornhill, the Minister of Development, and his senior staff to hear a presentation on a new tendering policy to be administered by Thornhill's department. Jerry Lawrence stayed for a few minutes and left while I sat through the presentation designed to change the long-standing public tendering policy of the government through giving a competitive advantage to Nova Scotia companies.

There was something not right, and more time would be needed to evaluate the proposal, especially given that no one in Government Services was consulted. Thornhill's takeover was in my view simply a scheme to expand patronage by expecting a kick-back from companies so supported. As a senior bureaucrat, I was not in a position to speak my mind to a powerful government minister, so I stalled for time to evaluate the new draft policy promising to get back to them.

Weeks later after not hearing from me, Rick Butler, the Senior Director, and mastermind behind the new policy came to my office for a meeting and laid out in more detail the specifics of the changes to be implemented. Sitting there silently my only thought was if I gave in on this the Department of Government Services would be taken over by the Department of Development and we would lose control of our mandate to supply common services across all departments, board, agencies of government following an open and transparent public tendering process.

When he finished his presentation, he was given the courtesy of raising and additional points and when there was nothing else, I looked him squarely in the eye and with a firm steady voice told him to 'get the fuck out of my office' and that was the end of it, the attempted takeover went no further.

Province House, which opened in 1819 to serve as the permanent meeting house of the Nova Scotia Legislature was built in the Palladian style emphasizing the symmetrical appearance and features of Greek or Roman temples. The building was in a state of disrepair with only cosmetic work carried out on the exterior since its competition. For years, the department carried maintenance money in the budget to look after patching and pointing work of the deteriorating sandstone and every year the budget was cut. The once stately grand building was showing its age and help was needed to get the funds appropriated to carry out the work.

In early 1985, while on my way to the Granville St. entrance to Province House the help arrived in the form of a brick sized piece of sandstone cornice which had fallen from the roof line onto sidewalk. Fortunately, the Premier was in his office and when shown the dislodged piece he immediately understood the consequences to his government had it struck a passerby and agreed that the Province House restoration would become a priority.

The Southwest Stone Cleaning and Restoration Company of Bristol England was hired to carry out a detailed assessment and submit a report and recommendation on the work to be completed to bring the building exterior to its original condition. The report recommended that the building be cleaned and a detailed inventory of defective stones be made. With this information, the Bristol company proposed to find a matching stone quarry in the United Kingdom, carve the replacement pieces and then return to Halifax to install them.

It was apparent that the restoration would take several years with no legacy benefit to Nova Scotia for the effort. There were several other public and private buildings with sandstone features in Halifax in a similar state of disrepair and unless a more local home-grown approach was conceived, many of those buildings would eventually be demolished. From these early discussions the germination of the idea to have Southwest Stone send over master stone restoration masons to train Nova Scotian apprentices to do the work under their tutelage became a reality. The training syllabus consisted of a combination of classroom and on-the-job training following which the graduates had to pass the tough London Guild examinations to become full-fledged journeymen of the stone restoration trade. To do this the trade had to be recognized by the Provincial Apprenticeship Training Board and receive the support of the Department of Higher Education and the Federal Skills Growth Fund training program. While these negotiations were underway, the quarry at Wallace Nova Scotia where the original sandstone came from was approached to supply the block stone that would be cut and shaped at a stone shop set up at the vacant Nova Scotia Power maintenance shops nearby at the foot of South Street in Halifax.

Setting up the program was not without challenges. The local masonry construction companies championed by Alexa McDonough, the leader of the New Democratic Party and daughter of Lloyd Shaw, the prominent supplier of masonry products did not support the plan. Her opposition to the British involvement especially in question period was relentless as she played to her local base of support, the masonry contractors and their unions who all were looking for a piece of the action.

To qualify for federal funding under the Skills Growth Fund an arm's length company was required to be set up. At a lunch meeting at a popular Halifax restaurant, I was joined by Don Power, Marc Cleary, a lawyer, and Chair of the Provincial Apprenticeship Training Board, and David Russe' the President of Southwest Stone and laid out the plan to set up an independent company to carry out the restoration and training program. It did not hurt that both Power and Cleary were good friends, and both had strong connections to the Premier who would give his blessing to the undertaking.

In February of 1985 Canstone was Incorporated with Marc Cleary named as president and sole shareholder. He was to be reimbursed for the actual costs for incorporating the company and for accounting services until such time that the company was on its feet and the shares would be transferred to the Brits.

The Department Government Services engaged Graeme Duffus a young architect specializing in heritage conservation to oversee and consult on the design and technical details of the project with the knowledge base of the master masons from Southwest Stone to fall back on, while department staff managed and administered the day-to-day operations including scheduling, budgeting, and procurement of all goods and services. Mark Cleary's office processed the Canstone cheques for the payment of approved invoices for which he was reimbursed for the administrative work plus a fee of five percent of the value of cheques written.

Power and I continued to meet from time to time, however not as frequently as we had in the early months following my appointment. In one of those meetings shortly after the restoration work was underway, he informed me that the five percent fee to Cleary on material purchases was to be raised to ten percent and this was to be paid on worker's wages as well. I objected strongly but was silenced when he made the statement…'this is what the Boss wants'… knowing that he was referring to the Premier, I bit my tongue and gave instructions to departmental staff to make it happen.

My meetings with Power became less and less frequent. The advice received was not always in alignment with my ethics and I reasoned that if I was going to have to answer for what I do, I could not very well use the argument that someone, being Power, told me to do it. The once strong bond and mutual respect we held for each other was quickly coming to an end and we both knew it.

Concurrently while the Province House restoration was underway preliminary planning had been finalized for the long-awaited new home for the Art Gallery of Nova Scotia to be built on a prime piece of waterfront real estate at the bottom of Sackville St. At the same time the newly completed World Trade and Convention Center had office space that they were trying to fill, and there was word on the street that the World Trade Center of which Power was a board member wanted the Art Gallery as a tenant.

Out of the blue, Peter Evans, the consultant hired by the Trade Center called wanting to meet with me to review the concept plans for how the gallery could be shoehorned into the vacant Trade Center space. It was clear that the concept was not feasible, however it was not a project that belonged to the Department of Government Services and not my place to object.

The reason I was made privy to the plan became clear a few days later when the Premier summoned me to his office to meet with the Art Gallery Board. It had been made public that the waterfront site promised for gallery's new home would be sold to the Premier's friend and former law partner Ralph Medjuck a prominent Halifax developer to build an office building that would house the law firm McInnes Cooper Robertson where the Premier's close confidant and advisor, Joe McDonald was a partner.

The meeting was underway when I arrived and the Premier was clearly not doing well with the board which was made up of some very prominent benefactors, the who's who of the elite in Nova Scotia. The Premier had just finished presenting the plan for the Art Gallery to be moved to the World Trade Center and went around the room looking for support. The board members, somber and clearly down hearted did not like what they were hearing and expressed their dissatisfaction in no uncertain terms. The Premier finally turned to me and asked what I thought.

As a back story, the Phase 1 of the stone restoration training program was wrapping up with the completion of Province House and Canstone needed other buildings to complete the curriculum required by the restoration guild in London for the students to graduate through the program and receive journeyman status. An ideal candidate was the vacant Dominion Building across the street from Province House which served as Post Office, Customs House, and Railway Department office for the former British Colony. When the call was received to attend the meeting, arrangements were made to unlock the side door to the building.

I told the Premier that I agreed with the board that the World Trade Center building was not the place for the Art Gallery. The Premier was clearly not pleased with that answer, however when the Dominion Building was offered as a more viable alternative - the resolution to his dilemma for reneging on the promised building site became clear. The mood of the meeting changed as we crossed the street and entered the historic building, an excellent example of late nineteenth century Italianate style architecture with exterior decorative sandstone elements including the statue of Britannica and the interior vaulted ceiling spaces with ornate architectural detailing. The board could clearly see potential here and the new home for the Art Gallery was found.

The board of the Art Gallery was happy as they have a new home that they can rally around and continue the fundraising campaign; the Premier was happy because the board was appeased and supportive of the way forward; Canstone and the stonemasons were happy because the training program could continue to completion; Peter Evans was happy because his company was appointed Project Manager for the Art Gallery of Nova Scotia project. The only person not happy was Don Power who lost a prime tenant for the World Trade Center.

Now that Phase 1 of the stone restoration program was ending, it was time to turn over the shares of Canstone to the British as per the agreement made when the company was first set up. The Department's lawyer Greg

Evans had drawn up the share transfer document to be signed by Mark Clearly at a meeting scheduled in early May 1987 at the boardroom of the World Trading Center.

Greg and I entered the room expecting to meet Cleary and were surprised to see that Don Power was there as well. At the meeting, Cleary, with the backing of Power, refused to sign without a commitment of a $30,000 payment. I argued that that was not the agreement that was set up when we met at Thackeray's restaurant some months earlier and that we will stick to that initial original agreement which was the basis upon which Canstone was conceived and to be operated.

The discussion became heated and Cleary let it slip that these instructions were coming from Buchanan. On hearing this Cleary and I huddled privately in the corner of the room and I said emphatically that I have no such instructions and that we can walk down the street to Province House to meet with the Premier because I wanted to hear his instructions from the horse's mouth directly. I told him that if this was in fact the Premier's instruction that I was prepared to submit my resignation.

Cleary capitulated and the share transfer agreement was signed thus completing the government's arm's length involvement with Canstone through Cleary as its President along with any kickbacks that he may have given or received in that role. The matter was not raised again by any of the players involved but I knew that I was walking on thin ice.

Dr. Mike Laffin a seat mate of Buchanan's in the 1967 Stanfield government was a tough, no-nonsense strong-willed Cape Breton from New Waterford, and the member of the Nova Scotia Legislature for the riding Cape Breton Centre. In November 1985 he was transferred by the Premier from the Department of Housing portfolio to the Department of Government Services to become my new Minister after the departure of Jerry Lawrence. Laffin was very supportive of the significant work carried out by the Department in several areas and we got along famously.

Besides the establishment of the stone restoration industry in Nova Scotia with the restoration of the historic Province House and Dominion Building, the growth in the capital budget increased from $35 million in

1985 to over $250 million in 1989 with the management of the design and construction of over two hundred capital projects.

The department also established a Central Services Building to accommodate an expanded Provincial Data Center with the growth of the provincial main frame computer capacity handling over seven hundred remote terminal connections managed by the Systems and Computer Services Division.

Every year a department was called upon to do a detailed review of spending estimates. In the spring session of 1988, Government Services were picked, and I knew it was a witch hunt as the opposition wanted to embarrass Minister Laffin who they felt did not have a handle on the rapid expansion and day-to-day operations of the department.

A duplicate set of briefing binders of the estimates were prepared with a copy for the Minister and after a few roll playing sessions he was as ready as he would ever be to defend the department's estimates. During the debate on the estimates, the Minister was located on the floor of the legislature with reference binders at his fingertips and I was sitting in the legislative gallery with the duplicate copies.

When an opposition member asked a question, I would write down the binder number, section and paragraph on a briefing note and have it sent down by a Legislative Page to the Minister below to refer to for the answer. It got to a point where a number of Legislative Pages were running up and down and the Minister along with the members below would when a question was asked, look up to me for the answer while waiting for the Page to deliver it.

To speed things up, the binder references were written on a card in large text and flashed to the Minister below. It was certainly an unorthodox approach, but it worked. The Minister got the estimates approved in fine form and was not once stumped by an opposition question.

In future years, the detailed review of all departmental estimates was held in the Red Room of Province House with the Minister supported by the Deputy and senior staff in attendance along with their briefing binders which were available for the scrutiny of the opposition parties.

CHAPTER 3

Rancid Pork in the Barrel

A significant amount of time and effort was occupied with the management of leases for government offices. Typically, office space requirements are managed by the Space Utilization Committee of the Provincial Management Board which was chaired by the Hon. George Moody. The requirement for office space was triggered by the need for additional space to accommodate a new program or service being provided by the government.

When Buchanan came to power the office rental space leased from the private sector was well under a million square feet at an average cost of $8.00 per square foot. Eight years later the province was renting 1.3 million square feet at an average cost of $17.00. The increase in rental space of forty-five percent resulting in the tripling of the total rental budget was directly attributable to Buchanan's patronage promises to major real estate developers.

One of the good old boys who benefited from the Premier's intervention in lease negotiations was Ben McCrae of the Armour Group who was the successful proponent in the development of the Founder's Square, on a block of land acquired by the Province in the 1970's and leased back to the developer over an 80-year period.

During the land-lease negotiations in the summer of 1983, McRae informed my predecessor Don Power that Founders Square would need a commitment to lease some 30,000 square feet from the Province to make his project viable. Power countered for an increase in the size of the building which would result in a higher return to the Province in land rent. McCrea was open to an increase in size if the Province would commit to lease 50,000 square feet of office space.

The proposal in principle was ratified by Buchanan and a cabinet committee giving Power authorization to finalize the office lease terms and conditions. McRae was looking for an office lease for the duration of the mortgage amortization period while Power was prepared to give a five-year lease with options to renew the term every fifth year at a rental rate to be negotiated.

Power initiated a new letter of agreement dated 4 October 1984 based on his terms which McRae signed. After he announced his retirement Power showed me the letter of agreement which I was given to understand finalized the negotiations with Founders Square respecting the Province taking space as a tenant.

In my early meetings with McRae, it was clear that he did not want to go along with the signed commitment letter, and with Power out of the picture, he felt he could get his way. The project was ready for the Province's promised 50,000 sq. ft. of government occupancy.

Buchanan, who made it possible for the project to get off the ground quarterbacked the lease negotiations to ensure that his friend got the terms he wanted. During these negotiations, McCrae would have no qualms in calling the Premier with me sitting across the desk to complain that I was being too tough.

In another session, two of the Premiers' assistants John McPherson and Dennis Ashworth were sent over to sit in on the negotiation and report back to Buchanan. McCrea applied pressure from all quarters including George Moody, the Chair of the Space Committee and Management Board who would ultimately have to endorse the final deal. Moody at a private lunch meeting added his voice to the pressure to conclude the negotiations on terms favorable to McCrae including having me agree to pay rent for space not yet occupied.

As a point of interest, Moody along with my Minister Mike Laffin and for that matter many members of the Provincial Legislature from outside of the city were tenants in McCrae's apartment building on the corner of South and Tower Rd. in Halifax. Evidently, I was expected to rubber stamp whatever was put in front of me and under such circumstances there was only so much that could be done to get the best deal for the taxpayer. Founders Square Limited ended up with a deal that would set the precedent for other developers to follow.

The next in line was Ralph Medjuck, one of the most highly favored of the Buchanan cronies. After promising Medjuck the waterfront site designated for the Art Gallery, Buchanan sweetened the deal by promising to lease space in the new building and no sooner had Cornwallis Place been completed the Department of Tourism was promptly moved in as flagship tenant.

Medjuck was followed by Yarmouth developer John Miller who was behind a deal trying to lease the vacant and rundown Morses Tea warehouse on Hollis Street to the province for use by the NS College of Art and Design. For more than two years he had been unsuccessful, then in 1986 he hired his friend Murdock Cranston to lobby government to get a deal in place.

Shortly thereafter, Terry Donahoe intervened on Miller's behalf and I was directed by Space Committee of Management Board to review the proposal. I told Miller that the empty warehouse was not worth the price he was asking unless substantial renovations and upgrades were made to bring the building up to current building code standards.

A counter proposal was offered on terms I was prepared to recommend to government and this led to unrelenting lobbying from several private sector leasing agents advocating on Miller's behalf. As the pressure intensified, I dug in my heels and did not budge until an acceptable deal was finalized – a deal which included a twenty-year term with an option to own for one dollar at the end.

The government approved the rate and term but would not agree to the ownership option. Shortly after the ink dried on the modified lease Miller flipped his interest in the property to a third party and pocketed a tidy return all at the taxpayer's expense.

Similar development incentives, whether needed or not, were handed out to Bob Stapells of Canterbury Investments to build One Government Place to accommodate government management and administrative offices including the Office of the Premier, Policy Board and Management Board; to John Lindsay for Purdy's Wharf, the iconic twin tower complex on the

Halifax Waterfront in which the government committed to occupy two floors in the highly priced Tower II for Department of Transportation; and to Mike Zatzman the son of prominent former mayor and community builder in Dartmouth for space in Alderney Gate to house the Department of Municipal affairs.

The ratio of government owned to privately owned lease space had grown to 30/70 in favor of the private sector. A plan was implemented to return the ratio to a more favorable position for the taxpayer by acquiring more of a share of the space occupied by government offices especially in the precinct of Province House. To achieve this goal, the purchase option in the One Government Place lease was exercised and negotiations were underway to acquire the Joseph Howe Building under a similar arrangement.

Since it's opening in 1974, the provincial government was the primary tenant of the Howe building located south of Province House on Prince St. and would likely remain so. Consequently, the province entered into a negotiation with Medjuck of Centennial Properties who were leasing agents for Confederation Life, the building owners, whereby the province would have an opportunity to acquire the building for one dollar at the end of the twenty-five-year lease.

The merits of the deal had been reviewed by the Auditor General's office who carried out a comparison of the two options; either continue leasing the building at market rates to be renegotiated every five years or establish a fixed rate for twenty-five years with an option of ownership. The AG concluded that the difference did not seem unreasonable in terms of eventual ownership.

The official opposition under their new leader Vince MacLean was hammering the government on the leasing file and I as Deputy Minister was offered up by the government controlled Public Accounts Committee to attend the session of late April 1988 to in essence, answer to the patronage riddled leasing activities of the Buchanan government.

MacLean, the MLA for Cape Breton South who was elected leader of the Nova Scotia Liberal Party in February of 1986 and was on a mission to expose government waste and corruption to pave his way into the premier's office by becoming the champion of government ethics.

At Public Accounts, MacLean was like a dog with a bone, hammering me for over two hours with his aggressive, and brutal grilling over the Buchanan government's leasing details on the Joseph Howe Building. During the questioning I refused to provide a copy of the lease, the details of which were protected by the Freedom of Information Act.

MacLean was not going to let himself be confused by the merits of the transaction which made no difference as his mind was made up - the government was hiding behind the Freedom Information Act to keep from revealing damning information about the deal with Centennial.

At the conclusion of the hearing, on my way out of the building the Premier who had been listening to the debate on a speaker in his office called me in to give me a pat on the back for how I handled myself under the relentless attack. The adversity faced at the Public Accounts emboldened me with the realization that I could handle myself under pressure by staying calm and trusting in my inner guidance.

It is interesting to note, that upon the completion of the twenty-five-year lease, the New Democratic Party in power took ownership of the building and then sold it to Universal Realty for $15 million with a commitment to continue renting space in the building for government offices. The private sector participation in and control of the long-term government leasing market is firmly entrenched no matter what party is in power.

After the closing of the legislative session Minister Laffin and I made a trip to Britain to meet with David Russe the president of Southwest Stone to tour some of the projects that they had underway, in and around the Bristol and Bath area of England along with a major project in Dublin Ireland.

Our Dublin itinerary had a free day, in which we took an early morning walk along the Grand Canal and looked across to see the Canadian embassy and on the spur of the moment, decided to drop in to present our credentials.

The ambassador was not there, however the Under Secretary for Trade received us as honored dignitaries. Upon finding out that Dr. Laffin was a Minister of Her Majesty's Government representing the town of New Waterford Nova Scotia he made a few calls and in short order had set up a private tour of the world-famous Waterford Crystal factory in Waterford Ireland followed by a luncheon.

An embassy chauffeured limousine was placed at our disposal and we had a full day of the royal treatment, the highlight of our trip. The following day we would be guests of Donald M. Smith, a political pal of Mike Laffin, who was Nova Scotia's Agent General in London for lunch at his club on the Pall Mall.

A short time after our return, Mike Laffin along with his conservative Cape Breton MLA colleagues were at a meeting with the Premier in the Cabinet Room. At the meeting, Rocca Construction a company from St. John New Brunswick was making yet another presentation on the development of the Sydney waterfront with the addition of the proposed new Cape Breton Regional Hospital as the anchor project.

The development was a political hot potato that was in the pot since 1984 and was now on simmer because the funding parties primarily the Federal Liberals lead by the newly elected MP Russel MacLellan and Provincial Conservatives with Buchanan calling the shots could not come to agreement. The City of Sydney with Manning MacDonald as Mayor and Vince MacLean the MLA and Leader of the Opposition were frustrated with the stalemate.

I was called into the meeting no doubt on the insistence of my minister. Upon arrival, the presentation with slick concept renderings placed on easels set up in the cabinet room was underway. At the completion, the Premier went around the room asking the opinion of his Cape Breton members, who were all in agreement that Rocca backed waterfront development project which now was to include the regional hospital should go ahead.

Perhaps they were so used to falling in line, they were reluctant to go against the Premier's wishes and went along with what appeared to be a fait accompli. As the meeting was winding down, the Premier turned to me and asked for my opinion, Speaking as an engineer it was pointed out that the infrastructure improvements to support such a development were significant and that a great deal more taxpayer expenditure will be required to make this a viable solution; moreover, the site left no room for any future hospital expansion.

I was not against the development of the Sydney waterfront; I was against the hospital being part of that development. It was my recommendation that the hospital be built on the green field site of several acres at the southwest corner of the interchange with the Mira Road and Sydney-Glace Bay highway acquired some years ago for that purpose, a site easily accessible to the Cape Breton communities that the hospital was intended to serve. Following my comments, the Premier abruptly adjourned the meeting without further discussion.

A short time later I happened to find myself invited to ride in the back seat of a car with the Premier returning from a government function. We chatted about several topics, however the reason I believe he wanted to talk was to confirm that the Cape Breton Regional Hospital should be built on the originally designated Mira Road site. That meant that Rocca's Sydney waterfront development project would be placed on the back burner yet again.

As an appeasement, the Premier wanted Rocca involved as the construction managers for the $80 million project and asked if I would have any objection. I stated that I could see no problem with the appointment being made. After all a precedent had been set with the appointment of Don Power to provide management services for the Halifax Infirmary Hospital complex, an appointment for which no other candidates were considered.

The award of the management contract was made as directed to Rocca, through their subsidiary Urban Consultants, with the understanding that competitive tendering of trade contract work would follow the normal policies established by government. The next day, I was invited to lunch with Fred Dixon, principal political confident of the Premier and a senior partner with Patterson Kitz, a prominent regional law firm with a head office in Halifax. At our lunch meeting, Dixon advocated for and promoted the abilities of John Rocca and the Rocca Group over and above very capable Nova Scotia companies with similar background and experience This confirmed my clear impression that the Premier wasn't calling the shots and that there were people in the shadows such as Dixon who were telling him what to do. After all the appointment of a New Brunswick company has no apparent benefit to the people Nove Scotia.

The local Rosicrucian group held a family-oriented Thanksgiving function in 1988 that drew members from across the region. Glenn Hannam and his wife Alexandra arrived from Sydney Nova Scotia. Glenn was a professional engineer working in the construction industry for Federal Public Works in Sydney. I had mentioned that Government Services will be looking for a Project Coordinator working out of Sydney on the Cape Breton Regional Hospital and asked if he was interested in applying for the position.

His resume was forwarded and reviewed along with others and subsequently vetted through the Civil Service Commission and he was offered an employment contract, approved by Management Board, which he accepted. Glenn was to represent the department's interests with the hospital working groups along with the Department of Health in the Sydney area and oversee the activities of Urban Consultants.

On one of my business trips to Cape Breton in early 1989 Glenn mentioned that his wife did psychic readings. I showed an interest and arrangements were made for me to visit their home for a session. Alexandra was a gifted psychic medium with a column in the local newspapers on dream interpretations.

Using the tarot cards as the introduction to the session Alexandra informed me that my higher self and several spirit guides are working closely with me. It was like shining a light in a dark room and so much more of what I was sensing all along became apparent as to the nature of reality. I've always believed that there is more to life than we perceive through our five senses and was now getting a first-hand introduction of what that more might be. Alexandra and I made a strong connection. There was information shared that we had and spent many lives together in the past and this as well was something that I wanted to explore further. We both shared relationships with our spouses that one could best describe as platonic and so when a kindred spirit is met who vibrates to compatible frequencies a bond is made.

The planning work on the hospital was proceeding on schedule with the participation and input of several stakeholder groups. Following the submission of the preliminary Cape Breton Regional Hospital design plans to the Hospital Construction Planning Committee for approval the project was placed in limbo. Don Power, who retained his seat on the committee delayed the hospital plan from proceeding for at least three months, which was clearly in a conflict of interest.

After the completion of Veteran's Hospital, Power went on to become the Project Manager for the new Halifax Infirmary building, a key component of the QEII Hospital complex in Halifax. The Cape Breton Hospital plans were put on the back burner when they got to Mr. Power who wanted to see his Infirmary project go forward first. Power's delaying tactics would have succeeded only with the Buchanan's knowledge while Urban Consultants and others hired to advance the Cape Breton project were paid to twiddle their thumbs while waiting for government approval.

When the Premier called the election in the summer of 1988, he shortly thereafter announced that Mike Laffin decided to retire and would not be re offering. The excellent working relationship enjoyed with Dr. Laffin, a friend and champion, ended abruptly.

Knowing Mike Laffin, I had the distinct impression that the decision was made for him. Laffin was effectively put out to pasture and being the good and faithful political servant that he was he did not object.

With the campaign under full swing all parties promised to reform the way government operates by providing more openness and honesty to Nova Scotians. George Moody became the Minister of Government Services while still retaining his role as Chairman of Management Board. One of the first orders of business was to implement a new public tendering policy under which terms all offices and other space leased by government of 2500 square feet or more must go to public tender.

This newly adopted leasing policy was nothing more than an electioneering promise. Once the policy was adopted, exemptions were added to justify their plans to hand out lucrative incentives to prominent developers which essentially allowed them to continue business as usual – rewarding the big money doners at the taxpayers' expense.

Moody had scheduled a press briefing to outline the new policy when he received information that a whistle blower had leaked privileged information on a lease document with Centennial Properties, which would have to be dealt with right away.

I was in Upper Clements about 250 km away attending a meeting at the time when Moody contacted me to inform me of the revelation and let me know that the Lands and Forests helicopter was on the way to pick me up. Upon arrival at Halifax the copter landed at a waterfront parking and I was brought to the meeting room at the PC election headquarters where a number of the backroom boys along with Moody were plotting strategy.

At the government's press briefing room a block away in One Government Place, I sat at Moody's right hand while he made his presentation on the new tender policy for government leases which was followed by questions. Right off the bat the reporter with the manila envelope started peppering Moody about the lease terms and conditions contained in the leaked document which he held in his hand.

Moody deflected to me to provide the answers and my initial response was to request to look at the document. The wind was knocked out to the reporter's sails when I informed him that the document he had was not signed and did not represent the deal between Centennial and the Government and that the final negotiated deal contained terms much more favorable to the taxpayer. With this revelation the press briefing was concluded and a political tempest over government leases was averted.

The Conservatives went on to win the September 6, 1988, election with a slim majority, had they lost to the Liberals, their leader Vince MacLean would have seen to it that I was out of a job.

The day-to-day operation of the department got into full swing again in no time. Our mail messenger service working out of the top floor of the

Provincial Building, a government owned property directly across from the front entrance to Province House on Hollis Street, operated a small fleet of delivery vans which picked up and delivered interdepartmental mail and parcels amongst the government offices in the metropolitan area.

It was one of the functions that I was planning to improve the efficiency of by providing GPS tracking information to optimize the utilization of the fleet. The plan hit a dead end when the manager of the service informed me that the messengers also ran personal errands for the Buchanan family and the staff either handpicked or endorsed by Buchanan were non touchable, so I left it alone.

In late October I received an unexpected call from a female employee of the Department of Finance with offices in the same Provincial building. She insisted on maintaining her anonymity and informed me that she witnessed a mail messenger employee dealing drugs in the back stairwell and hung up without saying more.

My first call was to Norm Atkinson an ex RCMP officer who had worked in Security and Intelligence in both Toronto and Halifax before joining Public Works in 1978 as Director of Security for the Province under Don Power following Buchanan's victory in forming the government.

After meeting with Norm to summarize the anonymous call, he said, 'Leave it with me I will look after it.' Norm slow-walked the investigation and stonewalled giving me any update on what he uncovered. The matter died a slow death, but I was left with the impression that there was more to it that I was not to know about.

A second revelatory phone call came a couple of weeks later to my home one Sunday evening. Peter MacKeigan, a childhood friend and now a lawyer representing Piercy Supplies a large construction materials distributer called to inform me of discrepancies between purchase orders and delivery slips on a project being carried out by the department's construction group.

The Maintenance and Operations Division of the department maintained a staff of carpenters, plumbers, electrical and other skilled tradesmen to carry out work on government buildings. At the time they were working on interior renovations to the Provincial Law Courts on Spring Garden Rd.

Rather than get into the detail over the phone, Peter and I agreed to meet early the next day in my office to review his evidence. At our meeting he produced documents showing how a purchase order issued by our construction group purchasing agent would be amended after approval to increase quantities and add a second drop-off location prior to delivery. For example, if the initial purchase order was for forty sheets of plywood to be delivered to the courthouse project, our purchasing agent would call in to add an additional twenty sheets to be delivered to another location with all materials charged to the courthouse project.

With copies of the documents as evidence I called Atkinson along with the Division Manager and outlined the situation. It was agreed to bring in the employee and request an explanation. He was not at all apologetic and gave off an attitude of, 'don't be so naïve, this is the way it's done'. Under the circumstances I had no alternative but to suspend him while the matter was investigated. His parting words to me were, "If you pursue this, heads will roll."

My next call was to Gordie Coles the Deputy Attorney General, to inform him of what was up which resulted in a follow up meeting with my Minister George Moody and Ron Giffin the Attorney General and that was the last I heard of the matter. If there was a follow up investigation underway, it was news to me, as I received no request from either the RCMP or Halifax Police to give a statement.

In a matter of weeks, following these two incidents, I went from being a trusted advisor with a finger on the pulse of Government Services activities working within the highest levels of power to a pariah; a 'persona non grata'. My opinion was no longer consulted and my participation in day-to-day meetings, communications, and interactions amongst my colleague's and peers was not welcomed.

Political operatives with close ties to Buchanan and Moody were parachuted into the department as executive assistants and managers with the primary purpose of keeping an eye on my activities. There was a clear sense that I was being sidelined for not passing the loyalty tests set up to determine where my allegiance lay.

The anonymous call regarding drug dealing could easily have been ignored and the information on the misappropriation of building supplies brought to me by an individual who happened to have strong connections to the PC Party of Nova Scotia could have been handled much differently. In the weeks and months ahead more such tests would be faced.

In the fall of 1988, I received a call from John O'Brien, the Premier's Press Secretary asking me to investigate the purchase of a European designed toilet seats which includes a storage compartment containing a roll of plastic seat covers and a dispensing motor. At the push of a button, the motor removed a section of an 'unsterile' plastic sleeve while advancing a clean sterile plastic sleeve over the rim of the seat.

After a sample seat was dropped off for an assessment, I got back to O'Brien with the suggestion that we acquire a dozen or so of the seats and set up a trial at the provincially owned Victoria General Hospital to be overseen by the hospital's infectious control team.

That idea did not go over well and the 'ask to investigate' turned into an 'order to buy' with directions to issue a purchase order for two-hundred seats at a total cost of over fifty thousand dollars.

In early 1989 the seats were delivered to a storage room on the top floor of the Provincial Building adjacent to the mail messenger hangout where they sat before being moved to another storage location. Evidently, the provincial health department told the government to sit on the plan. Distributing the electric germ-stoppers could heighten fears that AIDS could be transmitted through toilet seats, a common misconception at the time. The toilet seats were never used.

In January 1989 Moody was out and Terry Donahoe along with retaining other ministerial responsibilities was in as Minister of Government Services. Donahoe and I met weekly to go over several files that the department was working on that either he should be aware of or be required to provide directions on. We discussed the list item by item and at the end of the review his consistent response was 'leave them with me, I'll get back to you'. The next week's list was longer with new issues added to the items not answered from the previous week. His inaction bogged down progress on a number of important initiatives and a new way of dealing with his procrastinations had to be implemented.

At the next meeting the items on the list were reviewed and for each item a plan of attack was developed for his consideration with a request for approval to proceed. In some cases, this would work but, in most cases, the 'leave them with me, I'll get back to you' reply was his response. Donahoe seemed to have little or no interest in the activities of the Department of Government Services so from then on, I would go over the list and review with Donahoe the decisions made and actions taken. In my view it is better to act decisively and apologize for it later than to seek an approval that may never come and risk a schedule delay and an inevitable increase in cost often associates with such important issues.

One of the time sensitive issues was the upgrade of the Provincial Data Centre run by the Department's Systems and Computer Services Division. The main frame computers that provide information technology support for government operations were in various facilities around the city, primarily on the ground floor of the Johnston Building with limited space and no room for expansion.

The government had taken over the former Nova Scotia Liquor Commission building on Young Street and set up a Central Services building to accommodate a new data center, Queens Printer, stationary stockroom and other common shops and services required to support the day-to-day operations of government. Proposal calls had been issued to upgrade the IT infrastructure including mainframes, switches, storage units and terminals all of which were to be headquartered in the newly renovated building.

IBM submitted the lowest and best proposal which included a price discount incentive if the award was made within certain time period. The Minister could not or would not commit.

With my signing authority as Deputy Minister confirmed by the department lawyer and financing in place through the budget allocation, I unilaterally signed a $20 million deal with IBM resulting in the growth of the provincial main frame computer capacity to handle over seven hundred remote terminal connections without a hitch.

The IBM executive responsible for the account subsequently confirmed that the Province had moved from the bottom ranked government run data facility in Canada to within the top three. Donahoe and the government were pleased with the eventual outcome – had it not worked out it that would have been a different story.

When I was first appointed to the Deputy Minister's position, a colleague in an equivalent role offered a valuable piece of advice. 'If possible, avoid travelling for any reason with your minister or any political figure as they will attempt to compromise you through alcohol, drugs or women in order to control you.'

That piece of advice was on my mind when I was required to travel to Newfoundland with Terry Donahoe and George Moody to meet with Premier Brian Peckford and other government officials in that province to compare their policies around government office space and leasing. That evening just as had been predicted, Donahoe and Moody took me for supper to a strip club where upon arrival I feigned a touch of flu, excused myself and headed back to the hotel.

The next 'honey pot' event occurred a short time later when a longtime associate, former neighbor, and a senior official in the Department of Development invited me to a function at a local service club in our hometown of Dartmouth.

To my surprise, as part of the on-stage entertainment, an attractive young woman performed a strip tease act which was the last thing I expected in a well-respected non-profit service organization. At the end of the act, my 'friend' vacated his seat to my right and the completely naked young lady came down from the stage and sat next to me. We exchanged small talk for a few minutes and knowing that this was a set-up that would not end well for me, I politely excused myself and left. To mitigate any rumors of reaching her ears, on arriving home, I immediately informed my wife of the incident. My wife seemed nonplused and our friend who we both knew well was out of my life.

Patronage had been an effective political tool for not only the Buchanan government but for the preceding Liberal governments as well. Old habits die hard and so did the government's interference in the hiring and promotion of civil servants which, for the most part, followed the rules and regulations of the Civil Service Commission.

Buchanan called from a holiday in Florida with instructions to promote a John Cleary for the vacant $55,000 a year position as the department's Director of Finance, a senior civil service position for which he was not qualified.

John Cleary was the son of Buchanan's friend Mark Cleary, the former Canstone President who happened to be in Florida with Buchanan at the time. Young Cleary who had previously been parachuted into the Finance Division as a Contracts Officer with a salary of about $36,000, was interviewed and a more qualified candidate was recommended by the civil service appointed interview board.

Against the Premier's wishes, I accepted the interview board's recommendation and awarded the position to the successful candidate. Shortly afterwards and as a matter of appeasement to the Premier, Cleary was given a newly created job as Manager of Capital Accounts with a salary of $41,000 without having to compete for it.

With the retirement of the incumbent, the Printing and Publishing Division of the department had an opening for an Executive Director. There were professionals within the department who in an open and transparent search could easily qualify and be great in that role. That did not matter to Terry Donahue who gave instructions to hire Lloyd McQueen a longtime McCurdy Printing employee and a Conservative Party Vice President. With the smell of the Cleary matter fresh in my nostrils, I was purposely dragging my heels on the file; however, the matter was quickly brought to a head when I received a call from Donahue who was in the Premier's office at the time and instructed me to immediately send over the McQueen employment contract for review by both. Within days, the employment contract was fully executed.

In the spring of 1989, the new leasing tendering policy was to be tested on a transaction of significant size. Tenders were called to move the Department of Municipal Affairs to a new space with the option to the current landlord Trizec Equities to upgrade the existing space.

Three bids were received with the best option being to keep the department in the Maritime Center a fourteen-story building on Barrington St. at the foot of Spring Garden Rd. Following the announcement of the publicly tendered results Ralph Medjuck office called indicating that Centennial Properties had another proposal that they want the department to consider to which I replied 'it's too late all the bids are in.'

Within hours I was instructed by Terry Donahoe to allow them to submit their alternative proposal. However, to maintain the integrity of the new tendering policy, all bidders were given the same opportunity. The retendering effort produced the same results; Medjuck was second lowest. I was summoned to the Premier's office where I met with both Buchanan and Donahoe to review the revised bid results. At that meeting the Premier, told me that the Minister of Municipal Affairs wants to move and that 'You know my wishes, I'll leave the decision up to you.' I knew exactly what his wishes were, he wanted the award to go to Medjuck. On returning to my office the contract, in compliance with the leasing policy, was awarded to Trizec, the low bidder.

I was an idealist, believing that as a public servant my job was to serve the public, however my political masters felt that my job was to serve them first and that they would determine what was best for the public. These two positions were irreconcilable, and it was clear that my time in government was quickly coming to an end. At a weekly meeting with Terry Donahue, I informed him that of my plans to leave government and said that as a young man I have a long career ahead and wanted to look for opportunities with different challenges in the private sector.

CHAPTER 4

Last Days at Home and Office

The friendship with Alexandra continued by phone for several weeks following our meeting in Sydney. In early May we planned to meet again to see where this friendship would go. I planned a business trip to the South Shore to inspect several projects in different stages of construction and invited Alexandra to join me. She took the train to Halifax, and we drove two hours to a private cottage at White Point Lodge where she settled in until I returned from my site construction visits.

That night I was introduced to the Ascended Master Lao Tsu a spirit guide who supported Alexandra in her private and public dream interpretation readings. I could see his visage clearly, as he presented himself in his etheric form as ancient Chinese with a long white beard and beautiful flowing silk robes with matching cap. He has been with me ever since and can be called upon to assist in my own dream interpretations.

The next day, Friday, in returning Alexandra to Halifax to catch the train she was very ill so I drove her home to Sydney, dropped her off and dead headed back to my home in Dartmouth arriving at 2:00 am the next Saturday morning. On arrival my older sister was with my wife and wanted an explanation as to why I was late. I told her it was none of her business and that now that I'm home she could leave. I told Patricia that I needed some extra time to sort out where my life was going and that I have decided to leave my government job.

She informed me that she had been in touch with my present boss

Terry Donahue and former boss Don Power and that the RCMP were called to look for me. This was a rather shocking revelation, why would these people agree to take these actions for a late arrival home from a business trip. My plans to leave government upset her because she was not so much concerned as to my happiness or fulfillment in my career as she was with social status and financial security as the wife of the Deputy Minister. Why would I want to give that up?

Later the next week I was in Montreal on a business trip to attend a conference on the Cooperation for Open Systems attended by several computer hardware and software suppliers and users related to establishing collaborative standards for working within the IT industry. My family were visiting her parents in Saint John NB where I was to drive from Halifax on my return and pick them up. I called her and told her I was too tired and other arrangements were made for her to get home.

The ruse allowed me to stay for the weekend. Alexandra flew to Montreal and we attended a Rosicrucian Convention at Place Ville Marie with a couple of thousand from around the world. At the convention, we met the Morrell family who were highly connected in the Order and relate to me that there was much for me to do in this lifetime. They knew of the budding relationship with Alexandra and offered us their family cottage near Brossard in the Eastern Townships of Quebec if ever a getaway was needed.

For some time now I have been given indications of several past lives, one of which was Francis of Assisi, which I was having difficulty in accepting. While on a walk in the city my skepticism was shared with Alexandra and I said that I was looking for a sign to help me accept this information. We happened at that very moment to be standing across from Mary Queen of the World Cathedral, topped by statues of the patron saints of thirteen parishes of Montreal when our attention was drawn to a large flock of birds flying into the air from behind the statue of Saint Francis. The synchronicity of that spontaneous happening helped me come to terms with a past life connection with Francis.

I was developing a heightened sense of awareness and getting very much in tune with my vibrations and following my gut instincts. As an example, while getting ready to leave our hotel and head to the airport, an overwhelming urge came over me to get out of the hotel and get out quickly. Within minutes we packed up and bolted out of the room and were on our way to the airport. It was later brought to my attention that Norm Atkinson was hot on my trail and sent to Montreal to intercept me.

In an effort to patch things up with Patricia a spur of the moment getaway to the Digby Pines Resort was planned. The atmosphere in the car was tense with very little communication between us. Patricia broke the ice less than an hour outside of the city telling me about a disturbing and vivid dream dealing with death and mutilation This was no surprise as she has phobias around dying and in an attempt to ease her mind, I told her that death was not such a traumatic experience if one accepts that the soul is immortal and that it is inevitable that we leave this life eventually.

This conversation when downhill from there as my words did nothing to alleviate her anxiety. I could not carry out this charade any longer and told that I wanted a separation. Patricia did not understand me, did not understand my interest in mysticism, spirituality, reincarnation, or in any way trying to come to know myself from a metaphysical perspective. Ironically, I credit Patricia, for introducing me to metaphysics with the psychic reading information she shared early in our marriage and Patricia's only brother that she is very close to also shares similar interests. Nevertheless, we were totally on different paths, and this was not sustainable for either of us. She wanted to go home, and we agreed to cut the trip short.

On the way back home, I wanted to take a short cut onto a secondary highway and got lost ending up on a dirt road. This panicked Patricia who thought I did it on purpose and planned to get rid of her. She only calmed down after I turned around and continued back on the main highway.

I dropped Patricia off and knew that there were no relatives or close friends to call upon to take me in and continue on my way to visit the Hannam family in Sydney.

Although Glen and his wife were separated, my showing up unannounced was not looked upon favorably. Before leaving I used his phone to contact our newfound Rosicrucian friend in Quebec to take him up on the offer of staying at his cottage. With that confirmed a return flight from Sydney to Montreal was booked. My next call was to my secretary who I informed that I was going to take some time off and asked that she notify the Minister and send a memo appointing Darrell

Hiltz, an Executive Director in the department as Acting Deputy Minister in my absence. I did not want to speak to Donahoe or Hiltz directly because I didn't trust either of them. With arrangements in place, we left on an overnight trip around the Cabot Trail and were on a flight the next morning.

Alexandra and were met at the Montreal Airport by Pierre Morrell who drove us to their cottage and gave us the Cook's tour of the area identifying hiking trails, grocery store and the like. Stopping at a banking machine to withdraw cash from my account my bank card was seized by the ATM with no funds dispersed and an onscreen message to contact my branch manager; fortunately, funds were available from a separate credit card account.

A few days were spent canoeing, hiking and generally relaxing while contemplating the next phase in my life and resolved not to continue in government service. Perhaps the stress of the rapidly changing events was too much for Alexandra's normally quiet, reclusive lifestyle. While away, she came down with another bout of stomach cramps and on the trip back Alexandra's symptoms intensified. In the end, we both realized and agreed that a long-term relationship was not in the cards.

Alexandra's estranged husband Glenn aware of our travel plans met us at the Sydney airport on our arrival on Monday June 19th and told me that 'All hell has broken loose.' and that he had been ordered by government to call them as soon as he knew my whereabouts. I told him to call them back right away and tell them what he knew. Glenn also told me that Norm Atkinson and others were searching for me.

When she got home, Alexandra went straight to bed, and Glenn and I had a long talk. I told Glenn of my plans to return to Halifax, reconcile with my wife and that sooner than later I would leave government but for the meantime would return to work. I thanked him for his understanding and support and implored him to reconcile his marriage as well. He allowed me to spend the night before heading back early the next morning and I thanked him for his understanding and support.

After our talk, I was out picking up a few things for my trip back the next day. While I was out, my brothers David and John showed up wanting to speak with me. Initially Glen did not want to let them in, however they did not want to leave and were eventually invited to wait for me inside.

When I did get back my brothers told me that they had returned a car to Sydney on behalf of a friend of theirs who owned a rental business and needed a drive back to Halifax. This was a cock-and-bull story if I ever heard one. Between the time of my arrival in the early afternoon to their arrival at the Hanam residence they had to have been in contact with government, arranged for a car and be given the Hanam home address, while making the four plus hour trip to Sydney. I went along with the plan to see where it took me and let them take my car with the understanding they would pick me up the next morning at 8:00 o'clock. Clearly, they wanted to control my options.

Rather than head straight back to Halifax we went for breakfast where they stalled for time waiting for the arrival of Greg Baker a family friend and former neighbor who happened to be my lawyer. Greg was picked up at the Sydney airport at about 10:00 and the four of us headed back to the city.

They seemed surprised with my willingness to go along with them, questioning me about my marriage and work. I expressed emphatically that it was my life and that they had no right to criticize me or interfere with the choices that I make and to cut off further conversation I settled back and closed my eyes to feign taking a nap.

As we got closer to Halifax, I informed them of my plan to reconcile with Patricia and take the time needed to save the marriage and suggested that I take over my car and asked each of them where they wanted to be dropped off.

The car was pulled over and they informed me that they were not taking me home; that Patricia was too afraid to be with me unless I agreed to have an outpatient assessment with a psychiatrist. Initially, this further interference angered me but knowing that firstly I was not a threat to my wife and could easily account for my actions and secondly that if I didn't agree the three of them could easily overpower me to make it happen, so I reluctantly went along.

Remarkably, my brother John had been able to set up an appointment that day with his friend Dr. Teehan who was awaiting my arrival to the Psychiatric Outpatient Department of the Abbie Lane Hospital in Halifax. This could only have happened with the support of the highest levels of government to pave the way – the Ministries of Health and Government Services and perhaps even the Premier's office.

CHAPTER 5

Of Sound Mind and Body

John accompanied me to Dr. Teehan's office and stayed for the initial interview expressing, so he claims, the family's concern for my mental wellbeing. John's list of uncharacteristic behavior included my interest in mysticism and the fact I was on the spiritual path that did not align with our Roman Catholic upbringing; that I was changing my diet to include more healthy wholesome selections which were uncharacteristic to the eating style of the family; that I felt I was on a mission; and that I had separated from my wife. None of this was firsthand knowledge as John and I were not close and had not seen each other in months. I could not believe what I was hearing nor that Dr. Teehan was buying into this charade of foolishness.

John had no idea of my involvement with the Catholic Church, nor the well documented mysticism associated within the organization. Nor evidently was he aware that I continued to practice my faith, go to mass, take the sacraments, and support the church. In the September 1984 Papal visit to Halifax of John Paul II, as an extra-curricular duty, I accepted the responsibility of looking after site coordination, traffic control and concessions; I served as a member of the Archdiocese Business and Finance Commission and at a parish level oversaw a major addition and alteration to St Clements Church in Dartmouth.

In response, I explained that I needed some time alone away from my wife to sort out the direction of my life and that at my age it could be attributable to a midlife crisis whereby many individuals contemplate the purpose and meaning of life. The only reason that I have agreed to come for this assessment was to pacify my wife and family so that I could get on with mending our marriage.

While expressing a desire to leave Dr. Teehan cut me off stating that I would be kept for an overnight assessment, and to protect my anonymity be sent to an out-of-province psychiatric hospital where I was to be placed under the care of his colleague Dr. Singh who would coordinate further assessments and treatment.

I vigorously objected, however was told I have no choice in the matter as the government plane is standing by to take me there and that the Department of Health has agreed to pay the out-of-province expenses. As suspected, clearly the plan was hatched to send me away before I even arrived; the forces against me were much greater than I realized and the extent to which the government would go to control me was shocking.

The only thing I could not understand at that point was why. One of the ways that I deal with such situations is to go with the flow and see where it takes me and under the circumstances ahead of me it was important to deal with what's in front of me, maintain my peace and equanimity and take things one step at a time.

Confined to a secure ward in the hospital and kept under constant supervision, I was interviewed by a Dr. Bernie who went along with the preconceived plan. It was not clear to me who the architects of this plan were but in time I was determined to find out.

That evening Patricia brought my two boys Joseph and Tony to see their father locked up in a psychiatric hospital. Based on what has transpired so far, I believed her ulterior motive was to show their father in a bad light to give credence to her position that I was mentally unsound with the fact of my incarceration to prove it. Nevertheless, the boys were loving and affectionate with me and both very talkative. I expressed to them that I would be away for a short time but will be returning soon.

The next morning Terry Donahue and Darryl Hiltz visited. We engaged in idle small talk; I gave Darryl the key to the government vehicle and upon leaving Donahue said not to worry about anything as my wife and family would be looked after. My only option now was to go for the assessment in order to convince my family, employer, and the doctors that there was no cause for concern regarding my behavior in the past few weeks.

At 2:00 PM on June 21ˢᵗ I was discharged from the Abbie Lane under the supervision of my brother David who accompanied me to the Homewood facility in Guelph Ontario. The government plane was not available, however David had tickets for a commercial flight to Toronto.

While boarding the plane and taking our seats, I noticed a government colleague and close friend of Buchanan's on the flight as well. Was Joe Clarke sent to provide back up for David or was this merely a coincidence? I said nothing to David, nor did I speak to Joe as I did not want to have to explain the purpose of my trip.

On landing, David rented a car and we drove the 100 kilometers to Guelph. On the drive there was a lot going through my mind as to what to expect at Homewood. David said to me 'We want you back the way you were, or we don't want you back at all.' I wondered to myself who the 'we' were that he was referring to and wondered if this was a Freudian slip signaling that in fact I would not be coming back?

I did not trust David's motives but did not confront him or show my hand. On arrival to Guelph, we stayed the night at a Journey's End and to pass time that evening took in the premier of the latest Batman movie.

Early the next day, upon arrival to Homewood, Dr. Teehan's friend Dr. Singh, was not available and I was directed to see Dr. Ferguson the Medical Director, who interviewed me in his office while one of the ward nurses sat in. I answered a wide range of questions openly and honestly and readily admitted my interest in mysticism which was evidently a concern to many.

We talked about some changes in my lifestyle which many saw as being uncharacteristic of me and upsetting to my family. I expressed the opinion that I was undergoing a midlife evaluation and wanted to assess my past and what is important and not important in all aspects of my life and determine how I want to move forward.

I discussed my plans to leave my position as Deputy Minister, a position that I had reached at a relatively young age and one that I could not see myself doing forever. As a young man with an entrepreneurial spirit, I wanted to try my hand in the private sector, a decision that I admitted that my family is concerned about.

We discussed my wife's difficulty in understanding my metaphysical interests and the realization that she was not comfortable with them. I expressed the belief that my wife and family have greatly overreacted to my interest in mysticism.

At the end of the lengthy and probing session Dr. Ferguson said that 'Based on this interview there is no reason for you being here. You are free to go.' To which I was inspired to reply, 'Doctor I am not leaving this facility until every test you would have carried out is conducted and I leave with a clean bill of mental health.'

He explained that it could take up to three weeks to line up all the appointments. I indicated my willingness to spend that time for a complete psychiatric evaluation and expressed that I consider my stay a government paid vacation. An ulterior motivation for my insistence on staying was that returning now would be like kicking the hornets' nest back home, who knows what they would try next.

Dr. Ferguson arranged for a medical examination the next day, followed by psychological assessment tests on Saturday, another psychiatric consultation with a Dr. Pond who shared my interest in reincarnation, and a consultation with Dr. Greenway for a complete psychological interview. A neurological consultation was added to complete the study to rule out any concern about an organic process. I was also referred to the chaplain to explore my spirituality in a little more depth.

Fortunately, I did not meet with Dr. Singh to carry out the other investigations as suggested by Dr. Teehan. As the saying goes; "A friend of my enemy is my enemy." and since Teehan was no friend of mine I did not think that Singh his colleague at Homewood through whom he arranged my transfer before seeing me would be either.

My fear of being sedated and confined indefinitely was further allayed when I was given full privileges and was not prescribed any medications.

The psychiatric appointment with Dr. Ron Pond was scheduled for Monday which gave me a weekend to kill. I spent the time becoming familiar with the facility and meeting other residents with whom the popular past time was playing cards.

David decided to stay a few more days following his one-on-one background interview with Karen Cassidy, a social worker. On Saturday we made a trip to Glen Abbey in Oakville and spent the day watching the play at the Canadian Open, we also drove around the Guelph countryside. Most days David would come by to play cards during visiting hours.

David's newfound interest in my care and well-being was uncharacteristic for him as back home our lives were on a totally different trajectory, only seeing each other occasionally at family get-togethers. David was somewhat of a political animal, having worked as an aide for several ministers under the previous NS Liberal government of Gerald Regan and knew well how the system operated. No doubt he was reporting back to his fellow conspirators Patricia, brother John, Donahoe and others.

The interview with Dr. Pond went well, touching on the same topics raised by Dr. Ferguson. When it was over, we talked about our shared interest in past lives and reincarnation. His offer to conduct a past life regression was accepted and scheduled for an afternoon a couple of days later when he had no appointments.

The session started with Dr. Pond asking me to relax and breathe calmly and deeply and imagine in my mind's eye being in a very peaceful forest glen on the grassy bank of a crystal-clear pond. He indicated that in the cosmic time and space have no boundaries, so my consciousness is free go wherever it wants to explore. He then suggested that I go back in time and space and stop at a particular time and tell me what images are coming through my imagination. Almost instantly I started describing what I was doing and where I was.

I described being back in the middle ages in an institution like a large library or monastery studying and developing philosophical concepts. The room I was in was more like a cell with stone block walls and slab floors just large enough for a bed, a desk, a few pieces of furniture and books.

Dr. Pond asked, 'Who are you?' The name that came forward was Thomas Aquinas. He then asked to speak to my Higher Self asking. What is the purpose of selecting this particular life for a review?' Up until now I had responded in my own voice; the answer to this question came through me in an authoritative voice with a deep timbre sound stating that, 'He (Michael) will by example and discipline change people's outlook and views on life and that he is capable of facing the challenges that lie ahead.

When it was over Dr. Pond asked about my impression and I indicated that the session was fascinating, and I was a little overwhelmed by the life that came forward, which has given me much to contemplate.

On the Thursday afternoon an in-depth psychological interview with Dr. Greenaway was held. She reviewed the assessment test results from the previous Saturday which indicated a deferred diagnosis with nothing conclusive.

In our discussions I admitted to being introspective and questioning, while outwardly conducting myself within the conventional and stereotypical roles held while at the same time being very innovative. We discussed my work as Deputy Minister in Nova Scotia and the many new programs and services implemented while in that role. I expressed that at this point in my career I could not see myself continuing in the civil service for the next twenty-five years.

Dr. Greenaway then wanted to probe my extended family dynamics. I shared that I was the third child and eldest boy in a family of fourteen children and described my family as close knit but not overly communicative. By this I meant that we do many things together including the celebration of all holidays, get together on weekends, and drop by casually during the week on a superficial basis but with no individual heart-to-heart discussions to share our deepest thoughts and emotions… at least not with me. I told her that my mother is living, and that my father died fourteen years ago and that I had been married for seventeen years with two children. We then concluded by discussing the occupations of my brothers and sisters.

Later in the week I had a follow-up visit from Dr. Ferguson who wanted to probe some of the information in the social history given by my brother David, particularly in reference to possible hallucinations and hearing voices which was all new to me.

I expressed surprise stating that at no time had I spoken to my brother about this and that any information that he had was conjecture or a fabrication from my wife. We discussed my belief in the importance of trusting one's intuition as a skill that needs considerable trial and error practice. Dr. Ferguson briefly mentioned the possibility of follow-up treatment in the Halifax area and I pointed out that unless there was an emotional disorder to be dealt with, there is no need for it, to which he agreed.

At the end of the session Dr. Ferguson mentioned that my wife called requesting he return the call and that she inquired if there was a possibility that I could be certified mentally ill so that she could obtain my medical disability pension. I told him that I spoke to my wife daily and was not informed that she was going to call him. I expressed a preference that he does not return the call saying that I would talk to her myself. I also mentioned wanting to have a copy of my complete medical record report at the time of discharge.

The final test to be carried out was an EEG which was not scheduled until late the next week which gave me some time to kill. My first order of business was to call Patricia about her call to Freguson. The call ended with me telling Patricia then I would be leaving my job, that the marriage was over, and that I will be filing for divorce when I return to Nova Scotia.

How could I possibly reconcile with someone who insisted that I undergo an outpatient assessment following a short breakup before agreeing to see me then once I consented wanted me institutionalized to obtain my medical disability pension before a diagnosis was even made.

The daily calls to her and my conversations with the boys from Homeward stopped at that point. Then I called Alexandra and her husband in Sydney and told them what had transpired since June 20th when I last saw them. Knowing that there would be no favorable reception for me at home I asked if they could put me up following my discharge.

I also knew that along with my marriage, my career in government was over. Certainly not in the way that I had planned as I had hoped to investigate and consider several options leading to a transition into the private sector. However, by the unprecedented support given to the calculated, overly dramatic, and emotional rantings of a woman scorned, I was in effect constructively dismissed. How could I possibly return to work and be effective with my subordinates, colleagues, and superiors with the question of my mental capacity hanging over my head. I knew that once I was accused of being crazy even though I had the papers to prove that I wasn't, the damage was done.

On Friday, the day before Canada Day, Homewood held an outdoor barbeque celebration on the grounds of the facility at which the administrator approached me and mentioned that I must be a very influential person to get into the facility on such short notice. He said that a lot of strings were pulled to get me in so quickly, which although he did not say I assumed were at the Ministerial level between Nova Scotia and Ontario Health Departments.

MICHAEL ZARESKI

To collaborate this nugget of information, I was chatting with one of the rehab patients over cake and ice cream who told me that her husband was on the Board of Directors of Homewood and that even with his connection it took her months to get a bed and she couldn't believe that I was admitted within days.

The next week was spent taking long walks into the city, going to the library, and used bookstores, reading, and playing cards with the residents, and generally resting and relaxing during my last few days at Homewood. On one of my walks, I came across a patient who evidently had gotten out unnoticed wondering aimlessly on the sidewalk and escorted her back to the back to the facility.

The neurologist could find nothing of concern in the EEG and I was informed by Dr. Ferguson that my discharge would be on Friday July 7th. He asked what I should tell the family if they called, and I told him to tell them that I will be discharged early the following week, which he agreed to do.

I was packed by mid-morning and ready to leave the facility when the head nurse came in with the envelope containing my medical records and said 'Mr. Zareski. I owe you an apology'. I replied, 'Whatever for, you and your staff have been not nothing but cordial and considerate to me my whole time at Homewood.' She responded that when I first came, she thought that the facade that I was presenting was going to quickly shatter after a few days and that they would be spending the rest of my life putting me back together again. She then said, 'You have proven me wrong; I wish you all the best.'

CHAPTER 6

The Scheming Continues

L uckily, I still had a government issued American Express card in my wallet that I used to purchase the plane ticket back to Nova Scotia. On the flight back I opened the medical records package and was pleased with the unanimous conclusions reached from each of the various assessments; I was leaving with a 'clean bill of mental health.' The Documents confirmed my position all along that I was completely normal and was perhaps going through midlife changes in my attitudes with no evidence of disturbance which suggested or in any way was indicative of any mental illness.

There were revelations contained within the medical records package that I had not been aware of and found to be disturbing. For example, my brother David told the social worker in his session with her that they (John, Greg, and David) didn't know what to expect with me and had a rope in the car in case I was hesitant to return home. He as much admitted that their intent was to kidnap me if I did not go to the Abbie Lane willingly. He also stated he was staying to help facilitate my "treatment" which verified that he had his mind made up as to my mental competency.

Of particular interest was the summation of the psychologist Dr. Greenway who noted that in my interviews I delivered information in a sincere fashion that did not seem to be histrionic in any way. She believed that there were probably many unresolved family issues that would not impede my progress towards growth. She noted that although I may hold some very unconventional views as far as spirituality or my attitudes toward life in terms of what my family finds acceptable this is in no way indicating any evidence of psychosis or impairment in reality testing.

In her opinion, although I may have been the designated patient in the very enmeshed family system, I did not seem to be the one who has the major problem and had been sent here inappropriately.

Arriving at the Hanam residence later that evening, I was disappointed to see no change in the relationship between Glen and his wife. It was evident that their marriage was over nevertheless Glen was very gracious and allowed me to stay.

We shared information on the unbelievable events that had transpired. Glen had been under considerable pressure and questioning by his superiors in government as to my activities and his support based on a strong ethical stance was exemplary under the circumstances.

I knew that I had a few pieces of the puzzle but not all of them and needed more information to build my case going forward. Glen shared with me the rumors around town, that I was a drug addict, a member of the devil worshipping cult and that I had taken off to California. He even showed me a newspaper article with words to that effect.

Within days Glen Hanam's government contract as Project Coordinator for the Cape Breton Regional Hospital was terminated. Glen, a capable and competent professional engineer with a lot of experience under his belt formed a private engineering consulting firm.

The opening lines from my favorite poem "If" by Rudyard Kipling were often brought to mind during these times.

> *If you can keep your head when all about you*
> *Are losing theirs and blaming it on you,*
> *If you can trust yourself when all men doubt you,*
> *But make allowance for their doubting too;*

I knew that the government was behind this smear campaign and that I would have to be very careful in putting my facts together so for the meantime I planned to lay low.

There were several fronts that had to be dealt with, with one of the first being my banking privileges. I contacted the manager of the Royal Bank branch in Dartmouth where I had an account and he indicated that the return of my bank card was out of his hands and that I would have to go to the Regional Vice President, which I did.

The vice president was nervous when talking to me and said the account had been frozen when my whereabouts were not known. I countered that the bank had the ability to easily track my transaction and asked if this is an action taken for all their clients who were travelling on vacation? I requested to know on whose authority this was carried out and if he had been in contact with government.

He would not answer, but I did eventually get my card back, which didn't make much difference as there was no money in the joint account. I subsequently found out that my salary cheque continued to be deposited to the shared home account, and the funds were immediately transferred to an account exclusively controlled by Patricia.

To follow up on my intention to file for divorce I contacted Nancy Bateman of Patterson Kitz who had the reputation of being one of the top divorce lawyers in Halifax. In reaching her by phone she informed me that her firm was representing my wife on whose behalf they will be filing a Petition for Divorce and that as soon as I have a lawyer to represent me as the Respondent to have them contact her directly. She also requested confirmation of my current living address for her files.

Finally, I asked if she could arrange to have my clothing and personal effects sent down to me. She obliged and a few days later two black plastic garbage bags of clothes were on the doorstep delivered by an employee of the Department of Government Services with a note on his business card regretting that he had missed me.

In opening the bags what was found were items that had been put aside to send to the Salvation Army and not what I asked for. Perhaps it was a good thing that I was not home as the individual who dropped them off was a black belt in martial arts. Why was the government involved; could this have been yet another attempt to have me brought back to Halifax? A follow up call was made and eventually a couple of suitcases were sent along; and I now had an expanded wardrobe for the first time in three months.

After much searching, I contacted Michael King of McInnes Cooper with whom an appointment for an interview at his offices on Lower Water Street in Halifax was made. Upon arrival I introduced myself to the receptionist and was directed to take a seat in the expansive waiting room until Mr. King came for me.

While waiting, I had the uncomfortable feeling that my presence in the building was not welcome, especially after Joe MacDonald saw me sitting there. Joe MacDonald was one of Buchanan's closest political associates, and a partner in the firm whose offices happened to be leased from the Premier's close friend Medjuck.

Eventually I was ushered to Mr. King's office and outlined my position. He did not want to take my case but did agree to represent me at no charge to make initial contact with Nancy Bateman to start the ball rolling - my search for legal representation continued.

On leaving Halifax, I decided at the spur of the moment to swing by the Abbie Lane to get a copy of my medical records. The clerk at the medical records department copied the file and I was required to go to Dr. Teehan's office to have him sign off on the release.

On entering his office one of the first things out of his mouth was, 'You cannot honestly believe that the way you are living is normal.' He as much as said that Homewood got it wrong and that I should have a further assessment.

Upon hearing that, I took the documents from his desk, stood up and with adrenaline pumping, started walking out of his office and out of the building as fast as I could. He chased me down the hall calling out that a further assessment was in the best interest of everybody, especially my wife so that she could have my disability pensions benefits to look after her and my boys.

There it was again, 'my medical disability pension' first brought up by Dr. Ferguson from a telephone message he received from Patricia, and now from Dr. Teehan. Perhaps this is what my former boss Donahoe had in mind when he told me not to worry, my wife and family will be looked after.

The Abbie Lane mental health examination results made very interesting reading indeed. Dr. Birnie's report documented that upon examination Mr. Zareski was neatly groomed and dressed in casual clothes and he was calm, confident, and cooperative with no signs of agitation.

He had good eye contact and thought form and speech was normal. The patient is very articulate. Though content - the patient was preoccupied with the fact that he was just going through a "midlife crisis". There is no evidence of delusions or obsessional thoughts. Mood was subjectively normal, no change. Objectively he was appropriate. There was no euphoria or depression. On cognitive testing the patient was oriented to time place and person recent and remote memory were normal. General information was normal, there was good attention to questions.

In the physical exam Mr. Zareski was noted as healthy looking cooperative male. He looked his stated age and was in no apparent distress. In summary it stated that there were no abnormalities found. The patient was remarkably normal.

The nursing observations similarly noted that I was calm, cooperative, with smiling verbalizations and coherent in context with the appropriate effect throughout.

Dr. Teehan's observations continued in the same vein. He described me as being dressed in smart casual clothes, tanned and healthy looking. Mr. Zareski has an engaging smile and is quite vigilant during the interview, responding very sharply to the outline of the events that were put to him by his brother and very much on his guard and defensive. However, he was quite composed and in control - argued reasonably and logically.

He avoided the discussion around religious matters mainly on the basis that the interviewer was not sophisticated enough in knowledge of mysticism including reincarnation to discuss them intelligently. He said however he would go into these matters quite happily with somebody who did have a deeper understanding of them.

He showed no disturbance in the form of speech, there was no rapidity and no pressure of speech and no flight of ideas. There were no clear-cut delusional ideas. In his report he indicated that possible diagnostic possibilities would include a delusional disorder of unspecified type; an organic delusional disorder; or an atypical mood disorder.

Dr. Teehan's report concluded as follows, "I have arranged his admission to this hospital with a view to a transfer out-of-province to protect his privacy. He is agreeable to this plan, based on his own realization that those involved in his life are unanimous in feeling that he needs to have investigation and possibly treatment."

Nothing could be further from the truth. I was told that I had no choice in the matter as the government has already made arrangements for me to be sent out-of-province. Under the circumstances and with the forces against me there was no choice but to go along with the plan or risk being sedated and forced to go. My internal guidance helped me maintain a sense of calmness throughout which kept me fully vigilant with a heightened sense of awareness every step of the way.

Dr. Teehan had jumped to conclusions about my state of mind primarily based on secondhand information from several family and government sources who must have been in contact with him well in advance of my arrival.

There certainly was nothing in the medical reports of anyone that interviewed me at Abbie Lane to indicate that I was presenting in any way other than normal. I believe the report supports the plan for my assessment and eventual transfer to Homewood had been in the works for quite some time and that the intended outcome was to discredit me by having me committed for long term treatment.

Armed with the information from both Homewood and Abbie Lane, a complaint was filed with the Nova Scotia Medical Society regarding the actions of both Dr. Teehan and Dr. Bernie for having me sent away for an out-of-province treatment unnecessarily, thus causing great harm to my reputation. The report was well documented and supported by the records now in my possession.

I was pleasantly surprised a couple of weeks later when I received a letter back from the Registrar of the board stating that there were grounds for a hearing and that his office would be in contact with me to establish a date and go over other particulars. My spirits were buoyed believing that the injustices caused to me would be made right with vindication to follow.

Less than a week later another letter was received from the Registrar which now stated that there were no grounds for a hearing and the case would not go ahead. The second letter made no reference to the earlier communication as if the first letter did not exist.

Clearly this was the work of the government who have no doubt gotten to the Register when word got out of the planned hearing. Another indication of how pervasive and sinister the plan to silence me has gone.

At the time I had no idea what threat I was to government for simply expressing a plan to the change my career and try my hand in the private sector. Did I know something that I was not supposed to know, or did they think I knew something and we're afraid of me spilling the beans?

The next plan of attack was to go after my lawyer Greg Baker by writing a letter of complaint to the Nova Scotia Barristers' Society regarding his collaboration in having me "kidnapped" and forced to take and unwanted psychiatric examination based on the hearsay and prompting of others. In my view he should have defended my interests and informed me of my rights, and at the very least not got involved.

The response back from the Barristers' Society was that in their view there was no cause for disciplinary action and as far as they were concerned the matter was closed. This was not a surprise based on what had transpired with the Medical Board. At least now, for what it's worth, those involved know my position.

By now my location in Sydney was well known and in mid-August, my brother David and a former neighbor Barry McFarland showed up at the door wanting me to return to Dartmouth with them to see the boys.

As I had no money or no place to go that I could feel comfortable I asked if arrangements could be made for the boys to visit me in Cape Breton, an idea that they both flatly refused to consider, or pass on to the boys. At the time I had hoped that I would be able to see the boys in about two weeks subject to availability of funding.

The next emissary was Cass Williams the neighbor who introduced me to the Rosicrucian Order. I shared with him what had transpired, and that Patricia had filed for divorce. I expressed that my biggest concern was not having the ability to communicate with my sons. Tentatively arrangements were made for me to visit the boys on the condition that Patricia would release a small amount of my salary which she was now in control of to pay for travel expenses - a plan she refused to go along with.

By this time phone contact had been made with several of my siblings, some of whom knew what I was up against and privately kept an open line of communication with me. One of my strongest allies was my sister Mary.

As single young women, Mary and Patricia happened to live in the same rooming house on Jubilee Road in Halifax where they got to know each other, and it was no secret within family circles that Mary had little time for Patricia.

While I was dating Patricia, Mary was being courted by Donnie Brown, the brother of Garnet Brown a prominent businessman and former minister in the Liberal government of Gerry Regan. My brother David was a political aide to Garnet and maintained a close personal connection looking upon him as a surrogate father.

I shared with Mary the information from David about the rope in the car and she told me that they also had a syringe with a sedative that they were prepared to use if necessary. She also informed me that Bob Dauphinee a close associate of Garnet Brown with connections to the Royal Bank arranged for the freezing of my bank account and that Don Power had approached James Hayes, the Archbishop of Halifax to have me excommunicated and was turned down.

Other close connections included Don Power who was Brown's Deputy Minister when Brown was Minister of Public Works under the previous Liberal government of Gerry Regan and John Buchanan who entered politics at the same time and succeeded Brown as Minister of Public Works when the Conservatives came to power. Buchanan and Brown maintained a close social connection until Brown's death in 2010 – 'politics makes strange bedfellow'.

I was especially grateful to my single sisters Chrissy and Jackie who offered a place to stay any time that I was in the city. In numerous telephone calls, letters and visits with family members and friends the boys were always the number one topic.

Knowing that Patricia had hired a lawyer, I felt that I must have a lawyer to negotiate access with the boys. I did not want to hurt them any more than they already were by having them experience or witness an unfriendly confrontation between their mother and me. I did not want them in the middle of this and therefore held off on contacting them until I could do so under the advice of the divorce lawyer familiar with such matters.

In late summer I received a call from John MacEachern MLA from Glace Bay and the justice critic for the opposition Liberal Party. He tracked me down and wanted to know what was going on, and I cautiously gave him a broad outline of what had transpired.

He knew that I was still on salary and wanted to know why I was not in the office. I replied that because of the participation and cooperation of the government in conspiring with my family to have me sent out-of-province for an unwarranted psychiatric assessment that I was effectively and constructively dismissed.

Following that call I was contacted by my boss, Terry Donahoe, and arrangements were made to meet both he and Darrel Hiltz, the Acting Deputy Minister at the government cabinet office in Sydney.

Donahoe initially asked if I would consider coming back to work. Given the circumstances around the unjustified participation of the government in recent events along with vague and unfounded accusations of poor performance, especially where authority and respect of colleagues had been seriously undermined and compromised, I reiterated my position that I was effectively and constructively dismissed.

Donahoe knew full well that this would be my answer as there was no doubt that he was told as much by John MacEachern. With this response papers were presented for me to sign stating that I had resigned from my position, which effectively resulted in Patricia no longer receiving my salary.

I was agreeable; however I wanted to receive expense account reimbursements due do to me for government business conducted while I was still employed. The expense claim was made but never paid, however I was now able to apply for and receive unemployment insurance benefits which helped support me through this time.

Within days of my resignation, a position was arranged through Don Power's intervention for Patricia to be employed as an Occupational Therapist Aide in the new Camp Hill Hospital. Again, as Donahoe had said, my wife and family would be looked after by the government.

CHAPTER 7

Divorce Trial Avoided

In early October, Michael King agreed to meet with me in Halifax and go over the particulars of my case. He again reiterated his position that his involvement would be minimal. My priority with him was to negotiate access with the boys, however he did not accomplish much in this regard.

The next day I stopped by the Department of Finance and met with Al Manual, the Deputy Minister, asking if I could withdraw funds from my pension contributions. Although under any other circumstances this would have been simply a matter of filling out the proper documentation; but in this case he would not comply with my request.

I then crossed the street to Province House and went into the Premier's office and told them what I was looking for. Buchanan was taken aback by my boldness and asked me to consider coming back to work in the government. He was obviously nervous when I said, how could I, given the government's involvement in having me sent away to question the state of my mental health? He said he didn't know anything about it, and I came back with it could not have been done without your involvement at which point he admitted that it was only done at the request of my brother John who had called him on behalf of the family.

At the end of the short meeting the Premier called Al Manuel's office and arrangements were made for me to receive a cheque in the amount of five thousand dollars. A couple of hours later with the cheque in hand I headed back to Sydney.

In less than twenty-four hours Michael King called to let me know that Patricia's lawyer had filed an injunction and received a Court Order preventing me from making application for and/or receiving payments from my superannuation or pension contributions. King told me that he was aware of the conversation that I had with the Premier with respect to this matter from my wife's lawyer.

A few days later, I found out that Michael King met with Patricia, solicitor, and had no objection to extending the order for an indefinite period which was then ratified by a further Order of the Court. Shortly thereafter he resigned as my legal counsel. With access to funds frozen, no income, unable to afford a lawyer, ineligible for legal aid, I was on my own again dealing directly with Patricia's lawyer without counsel. I knew that I was in a in an extremely vulnerable position and therefore could not effectively proceed with my main issue of access to my children.

In the late afternoon on November 1st a knock came to the back door of the Hanam residence where I was staying. Rick Grant of ATV News along with his cameraman man with tape rolling said that he had heard rumors that I was a part of a devil worshiping cult and wanted to talk to me about it.

I would not agree to open the door but did agree to be interviewed at the Holiday Inn the next day. On arriving at the room where the interview would take place the cameraman was positioned behind the tripod, and I was directed the sit in a chair across from Rick Grant.

In such situations, I found that the best way to conduct myself was to imagine being in a column of white protective light, like what you would have seen in a Star Wars movie, then to ask that my Guides and Guardian Angels be with me. When asked a question I would pause, check for internal guidance, then calmly and peacefully give the answer.

The interview went on for an hour and a half and covered a wide range of topics from my leaving government; to the rumor that I was a drug addict and part of a cult and had taken off to California; the Rosicrucian Order; and the circumstances around my out-of-province assessment at Homewood in Guelph Ontario.

There was not one question that was asked that was not fully and completely answered. To the suggestion that the Rosicrucian Order was a devil worshipping cult I pointed out that the AMORC organization that I belong to was made-up of like-minded men and women from all over the world who we're interested in the study of mysticism science and the arts and had a sincere interest in the meaning and purpose of life, searching for answers to the age-old questions; 'Who are we? Where do we come from? Why are we here?' I also pointed out to him that there was a strong connection with Freemasonry with many Masonic Lodges having a Rosicrucian degree and that many Rosicrucians are as well Freemasons.

The rumor mill about the devil worshiping cult was effectively quashed. The suggestion that I was a drug addict was dispelled by the obvious state of good health and wellbeing that I projected along with my stated aversion to drugs of any kind including pharmaceuticals and my belief in natural remedies along with eating heathy wholesome food.

The interview concluded with him asking me if I had a message for anyone and I told him that I wanted my sons to know the love and concern that I have for them. Before leaving, the cameraman shared his anxiety that this was going to be the scariest interview that he ever conducted and that after meeting and listening to me he was very much put at ease.

The next day with much anticipation, I turned on the ATV Evening News only to see that the hour and a half interview was distilled into a three-minute segment saying basically that the former deputy minister is no longer working with government and is living in Sydney NS., with no message for my sons.

The rumor that I was a drug addict confused me and I wondered why this what being spread around. The answer came a few weeks later while attending a Natural Healing and Health fair in Sydney. One of the booths offering services was an Iridologist and I took advantage of a free session.

After looking at my irises, she asked what drugs I was on. I said I am not on any drugs I don't even take an aspirin to which she replied your eyes are telling me that there are definitely drugs in your system. Reflecting back to my last weeks in government, a temporary secretary had been assigned to me who happened to have been Don Power's former secretary for many years would have a cup of coffee on my desk every morning on my arrival.

I was not a coffee drinker but did accept it. I now questioned in my mind perhaps was I being drugged and didn't know it? My strict regime of meditation, eating healthy, walking, breathing exercises and raising my consciousness perhaps mitigated the effects of the drugs and this clearly must have confounded the instigators of the rumour.

Although Michael King was off the case, in early December I called and asked him to contact Patricia's lawyer to see what arrangement could be made for me to see the boy before Christmas and a couple of weeks later Bateman replied that the boys would require psychological assessment and counseling before they could see me - another stall tactic and roadblock to overcome.

My next attempt to communicate with my boys came with help from my sister who set up a time to call my mother's home on Christmas Day to speak to them while they were visiting. At the prearranged time the call was made but the boys had gone home.

With no legal representative, on the 23rd of January I made a trip to Halifax and filed an application to the court to have the order blocking me from accessing my pension contributions dated October 11th 1989 discontinued. This would allow me to make application for and receive my full pension contributions that have been withheld based on misleading information contained in the Patricia's affidavit. The funds I argued will also be applied against matrimonial debts as listed in the statement of property and also be used to provide the necessary retainer to engage a lawyer. Needless to say, my request was objected to by Patricia's lawyers.

I decided that before heading back to Sydney to stop by my home in Dartmouth to see the boys. My youngest son Tony came to the door and the look of fear in his eyes on seeing me was heart wrenching.

I was allowed as far as the kitchen, the boys were sent to their rooms and told not to come down. My brother David and neighbor Barry McFarlane who, five months ago, wanted me to come back with them to see the boys were then called to the house by my wife to ensure that I left without seeing them.

Not wanting to provoke the situation further and seeing the obvious control Patricia wielded, I left quietly. Before leaving I wrote a note addressed to the boys expressing my profound love for them, and hoped it was received.

My further attempts to contact the boys in the following weeks were not successful. There was hope on the horizon for legal representation in late February when contact was made with Douglas Stevenson of Rockwell,

Moore who was willing to take my case subject to my ability to come up with a retainer.

In the meantime, I was still dealing with Patricia's lawyer and through her was informed that Dr. Teehan, the psychiatrist who attempted to have me certified and who had been treating Patricia was chosen to carry out the assessment on the boys and concluded that the boys do not have to see me if they don't want to.

Pursuant to the court application made late January, and after much back and forth between Bateman and Stephenson an arrangement was made through a Court Order whereby funds would be released from my superannuation account to pay Stevenson's retainer and an additional amount would be released to Patricia to bring the mortgage payment on the matrimonial home out of arrears.

With Stevenson on board, he was very busy on several fronts throughout the month of May. An agreement was reached whereby Mrs. Zareski would not oppose the children seeing me as long as either of my brothers John or David was in attendance and the children wished to do so.

Several attempts were made over the next few weeks by both Stevenson and me to contact both John and David to assist in this regard with no success. In a call to David, he basically told me that I do not deserve to see the boys and that he would not help, and John would not return my calls.

Stevenson expressed an objection to the use of the Dr. Teehan's report at trial for obvious reasons and was attempting to engage an independent third-party to carry out an assessment of the boys related to access however cost sharing could not be arranged and this had to be postponed due to my lack of funds. As well we had to prepare for and attend discoveries at the end of the month in order to get ready for the divorce trial.

At the discovery hearing Patricia was represented by her lawyer Nancy Bateman and her assistant Jan Chisolm who drilled through a long list of questions for several hours going over in minute detail my actions leading up to an including my separation from Patricia for the purpose of locking down what evidence I had and the testimony that I would be expected to give. During the hearing they were informed that my medical records which contradicted her claim of my mental incompetence would be submitted as evidence with a copy provided to them with the agreement that the records are to be kept private and confidential and would be sealed by a Court Order.

Later in the day Doug Stevenson had his turn to question Patricia and was able to obtain context and clarity for much of the testimony included in her affidavit in support of her petition for divorce of 15 August 1989. It was noted that although the affidavit was accepted by the court it was not signed by Patricia or sworn to by her lawyer.

The questioning around who she was in contact with in government during my absence from home revealed the names of both Terry Donahoe and Don Power. When asked if she had been in contact with Buchanan at this time, she answered no.

Later, the questioning pivoted to the Court Order of October 6th blocking me from obtaining further pension funds a day after I had met with Buchanan who facilitated me receiving a cheque on October 5th. She was pressed hard on how she found out and claimed that she had promised not to say and after further questioning started to imply the government and Buchanan's involvement. Before she could go any further and much to our surprise Nancy Bateman stopped her testimony and agreed to settle.

The remaining of the session involved the drafting of the Minutes of Settlement between the Parties which among other things included the following provisions. In lieu of monthly maintenance and support payments, I would make a lump sum contribution equal to the value of the remaining funds in the superannuation account.

The matrimonial home would be sold as expeditiously as possible under the sole control of Patricia and that would facilitate the sale of the property. The proceeds from the sale of the home would be split fifty/fifty between us and we were to share in the cost of mortgage payments while the house was on the market. It was also agreed that we would not incur any debt or liability for each other.

The most important clause in the settlement agreement centered around custody and access to the children. Because of my employment status and the indeterminant prospects of my circumstances turning around any time soon it was agreed that Patricia would have custody of the children with reasonable access given to me on reasonable notice subject to the wishes of the children. Furthermore, the children were to be told of my desire and right to have access with them.

Initially to assist the boys a member of the family was to be present and Patricia was to facilitate access by doing everything reasonable including forwarding written material and gifts from me. I was given right to have telephone access and be informed of any major events in their lives including progress in school and health records etcetera. Such information is to be provided through my family or directly from time to time.

It was mutually agreed that the re-establishment of the relationship was of paramount importance and in the best interest to the children. My desire to re-establish a relationship and pass on that the love I have for the boys has not diminished was to be conveyed by the mother to our sons.

Knowing how expensive legal fees can be in in preparation for a divorce case, especially one as contentious as this, I wondered to myself where Patricia came up with the money to cover her costs. This was never a point of discussion; and in her case, she had two lawyers representing her.

Could it be that she was being helped by the government who perhaps had a hand selecting and quarterbacking the Patterson Kitz team? After all, Fred Dixon, the Senior Partner in the firm had very strong ties with the Premier - it certainly was something for me to think about based on how quickly the questioning around the government's involvement in this case was stopped.

On March 31st the Consent Order was approved and filed by the Supreme Court. What could have turned into a messy and lengthy public divorce with the uncontested and well documented participation of the Nova Scotia government and other parties on behalf of Patricia was now behind me and I had hopes to now move on with my life.

As a fitting reward for exemplary and outstanding service in her family law practice, five weeks later Nancy Bateman moved on with her life being appointed to the bench as Nova Scotia's first female county court judge.

CHAPTER 8

Public Attack Begins

N o sooner had the ink on the divorce settlement dried when I received a letter from the secretary of the Standing Committee on Public Accounts of the Nova Scotia Legislature requesting my presence at the June 13th meeting to reviews public spending, reports, and other financial matters of the Department of Government Services.

This request in my view was very odd. I could not understand why the government who had full control over what issues would be brought before the Public Accounts Committee along with witnesses to be called would agree under the circumstances to have me as a disgruntled former Deputy Minister appear before them.

Surely all the information related to Government Services current activities was available from the Department and could be testified to by the current Deputy Minister Darrell Hiltz and John MacLean the Director of Property and Operations who both were called to appear. I was cautious but had no option but to agree to the summons.

No sooner was my presence confirmed when I received a call from Bernie Boudreau, a Liberal MLA from Cape Breton who left a message that he wanted to meet to prepare my answers to the questions that would be coming from the Liberal side. I did not return his call and to ensure that I was not influenced in any way prior to my attendance I stayed incommunicado and went into hiding for a few days.

The meeting convened at 9:00 am with brief introductions and with some housekeeping matters cleared up. Vince MacLean, Leader of the Opposition opened with a series of questions around the hiring of Lloyd McQueen to the position of Director of Publishing.

In my response I told him that in the fall of 1989, my minister George Moody asked that Mr. McQueen be interviewed for a Director's job in the publishing group of the department. I met with Mr. McQueen and explained that the department was currently planning a reorganization and that there would be nothing coming available until the new structure was approved.

In January Mr. Moody was transferred to another department and Terry Donahue became my minister and resurrected the interest in a contract for Lloyd MacQueen. I was dragging my heels perhaps a bit too long because a while later, Donahoe called from the Premier's office with instructions to immediately send over the McQueen contract for review. Shortly thereafter the contract was signed.

Mr. MacLean next asked if the Premier often takes a role in reference to activities within the Department of Government Services. When checking with my guides, I got the sense of what the answer would be and then internally asked 'Do you really want me to say what's coming?' and a mental response in the form of a thought would come back, 'Yes, go for it.'

To MacLean's question I replied it was my feeling, the Premier felt he was in fact the Minister of Government Services. It was a portfolio that he held when first in government and the Premier was very much in contact throughout my day-to-day activities as the Deputy Minister. I consulted with him on a variety of topics including construction tenders, leases, and the employment of individuals. I knew with that answer that the proverbial can of worms had been opened and the tenor of my responses going forward was established.

MacLean then probed deeper into leases and was told that the Premier was kept fully briefed and was certainly aware of the status as they progressed of all major lease and lease purchase negotiations. I testified that at times there were certain leases that the Premier was anxious to have concluded or moved along quickly and that since he was the Premier and I was a Deputy working in his government I was obliged to comply with his wishes. I explained that at times I felt pressured into a negotiation position and could have gotten better terms without that influence. With the pressure to move negotiations along I did the best I could under the circumstances.

The next line of questions from MacLean dealt with the award of tenders for schools and hospital construction, asking if the Premier took an active role in the award of these tenders. I responded that yes there were some tenders that the Premier was particularly interested in, and I recalled receiving a telephone call from the Premier asking me to award a contract to the second lowest bidder in a major hospital expansion program.

I resisted and subsequently made an adjustment to the tender documents and recalled them to give all bidders a fair and competitive second chance at the work. It came about that the Premier's choice was still the second lowest bidder and I then awarded the contract to the successful bidder and was verbally reprimanded for my action. Trying to do my best as a Deputy Minister to maintain the integrity of the department and the government was clearly not appreciated.

The next series of question came from Bernie Boudreau regarding the tendering process focusing on the contract award to Rocca Construction for the Cape Breton Regional Hospital to which I responded that this this was a sole source award made at the direction of the Premier.

Boudreau then went on to discuss the enriched retirement package given to Don Power, asking who was involved in negotiating this deal. He was told that that only the Premier and Power were involved and that I was aware of the negotiation but as a subordinate was not involved. It was made clear that the contract was signed between Power and the Minister of the Department of Government Services and that on a day-to-day basis there was no involvement of the department, including myself, with Mr. Power's activities.

Boudreau was told that at the completion of the Veterans Hospital project while waiting for approval from government to move forward with the much larger Camp Hill Health Center there were discussion between David Nantes, the Minister of Health, and my minister Terry Donahoe as to what should be done with Don Power.

They asked my opinion, and in concurrence with the direction of the discussion I replied that if his role and function was completed, his contract should be terminated. A short time after that conversation, Terry Donahue announced to the House of Assembly that "I expect before too much time passes, and I refer to periods of weeks as opposed to months. I think we will find that the arrangements with Mr. Power are brought to an end."

Questioning swung back to Vince MacLean zeroing in on the planning and development of the Cape Breton Regional Hospital in Sydney. The role and function of the Hospital Construction Planning Committee and the approval status of the project was explained. My testimony was that the project had arrived at the completion of the preliminary design stage, and it was necessary to receive the Committee's approval before going on to tendering and construction. MacLean was told that the project died after the plans were sent to Power and this could not have happened without the knowledge and consent of the Premier.

It was now the Governments' time with my former minister George Moody leading off by asking if in the last year since leaving government had any discussions been held with Mr. MacLean, Mr. Boudreau, or Mr. John MacEachern or any other of the Liberal members in Cape Breton. I informed him of discussions initiated by MacEachern about circumstances asking how he could help with respect to the actions of government with my private life. He was aware of some of the newspaper reports and other rumors that were rampant at the time and he wanted to reach out to get the story from the "horse's mouth".

Mr. Moody probed further asking me to elaborate on the rumors and I knew now where this was going. This leading question was designed to speak to my state of mind with the intention of discounting my testimony or anything else I had to say.

I responded by summarizing the circumstances around my psychiatric assessment at the Abbie Lane Hospital and the government's role in facilitating and out-of-province assessment to Homewood in Guelph Ontario.

John MacEachern was concerned with the rumour being spread around government that I had a mental breakdown and from the evidence that I have they did get involved and caused a lot of people to question whether I was crazy or not or whether I did have a nervous breakdown.

Mr. Moody's 'bullshit' response reinforced the theme of his questioning around rumors said that at the time he and his colleagues had a lot of concern for me, my family, and my health, and they did not know what they could do.

David Nantes, Minister of Health was up next probing the circumstance around the hiring of Glen Hanam as Project Coordinator for the Breton Regional Hospital Project. He was told that Mr. Hanam was hired under a contract approved by the Management Board on my recommendation. The tone of questioning was as if I was an opposition witness and then became silly and nonsensical.

MR. NANTES: I understand he used to spend an hour and a half a day standing on his head. Are you aware of that?

MR. ZARESKI: No. I do not even think he's aware of that.

MR. NANTES: That was never reported to you?

MR. ZARESKI: No.

MR. NANTES: It was never reported that he would go in his office and close the door and …

MR. ZARESKI: No, I have known Mr. Hanam subsequently to this and I have never seen him stand on his head.

MR. NANTES: There is a personal connection with you and Mr. Hanam isn't there?

MR. ZARESKI: I know Mr. Hanam well, yes.

MR. NANTES: There is a personal connection.

MR. ZARESKI: Well, how much more personal can you be by saying I know him well?

MR. NANTES: Well, I do not know, maybe you could explain. Is there a personal connection? Did you know him personally before you hired him?

MR. ZARESKI: I met him to interview him, that is how I came to know him.

MR. NANTES: I see, and did you maintain a contact with him? A business contact or what, business and social?

MR. ZARESKI: Business and a friendly contact, he is a friend of mine. Mr. Hanam happened to be one of the only people who seemed to be supporting me through this period of time, that I referred to Mr. Moody, where everything that I had was taken away from me.

MR. NANTES: So, it was not reported to you that he used to do his meditation for an hour and a half a day standing on his head in his office by himself?

MR. ZARESKI: No that was not reported to me.

MR. NANTES: You were not aware of that?

MR. ZARESKI: Could I ask you where you got the information from? I could check with your sources.

MR. NANTES: You do not recall that other people in the project related this to you? You had forgotten about that?

MR. ZARESKI: You give me the name of the person who related it to me, and you might refresh my memory, but I do not recall hearing about Mr. Hanam standing on his head. I know he bent over backwards to try to do a good job, but I do not think he could stand on his head.

I knew exactly the intent of the probing questions. Nantes wanted to make a connection between Glen Hanam and his estranged wife. The three of us shared an interest in mysticism and the Rosicrucian Order and they provided safe sanctuary when I left Homewood. Nantes was not bright enough to pose the questions in a way that would give him what he was looking for.

Nantes then went on to claim that shortly after I left government the hospital user committees for the Cape Breton project were very dissatisfied with the process and they felt that they had not been listened to and that a lot of the work would have to be redone.

It was pointed out to Nantes that if there was any dissatisfaction with the process by the hospital user committees the fault lay with the Department of Health who was in control of obtaining stakeholder approvals for the project.

The preliminary plans and specifications for the hospital were signed off by the user committees and the Department of Health while I was Deputy and forwarded to the Hospital Construction Management Committee where they were held up by Don Power.

Thinking about the situation afterwards it is my belief that the plans for the Cape Breton Hospital were changed after I left in order not to give credit to the state-of-the-art design approach carried out by the amalgamated team of users, designers and health care professionals under the guidance and direction of Government Services.

What the government ended up doing was scrapping those plans that incorporated innovative layouts giving the patients rooms views of the spacious greenfield site. The revised hospital design ended up being a multi-story rectangular box based on the design that Power was implementing for the Halifax Infirmary. After all the government could not very well go the lengths that they did to discredit me and question my mental competence and then give credit to a job well done.

Next, Darrel Hiltz received a series of lob-ball questions around the policies of the department related the leasing of government office space, to the selection of professional services, tendering and the applicable government services guidelines the answers to which he effectively knocked out of the park.

In Vince MacLean's second round, he made the statement that the whole patronage system seemed to be run directly by the Premier and he wondered if someone was being rewarded along the way. In probing further MacLean asked if I had a specific example of where patronage and kick back were involved.

With that question, the door was open, and I let the cat out of the bag to see where it would go telling him that there was a situation that I became very much involved with the process of reward for contracts and at the time being prepared to offer my resignation if it continued.

I then went into detail about the appointment and role of the Premier's close friend Mark Cleary as the President of Canstone. Cleary's role as the paper president was to incorporate the company and facilitate the payment of invoices for goods and services for which it was agreed to pay him a five percent fee for the value of the invoices processed. Shortly thereafter, at the direction of 'the Boss', communicated to me through Don Power, Cleary's fee was increased to ten percent across the board on all the work that flowed through Canstone including payroll cost.

As stipulated in the agreement with Cleary, when Canstone was mature his involvement would end, and the company would be turned over to the team that had in fact built the company. Cleary insisted on a $30,000 payment before he would agree to sign over his shares in the company and told me that this was not all for him and that this was something that he had discussed with the Premier. To which I said, well, Mr. Cleary, you and I can go down to the Premier's office and we will discuss it eyeball to eyeball. If directed by the Premier to pay, I was prepared to submit my resignation - Cleary signed the share transfer agreement.

MacLean dropped his line of questioning like a hot potato not wanting to pursue the topic of kickbacks for political favors. It was well known that the Liberal Party when they were in power, had a tollgate scheme in place whereby companies that did business with the Liberal government kicked back a percentage of the value of the work received. This was clearly a sensitive political issue, and the discussion went no further.

To change the topic, MacLean rehashed the lease purchase agreement negotiations with Ralph Medjuck for the Joe Howe building, a subject that had been thoroughly beat to death at a Public Accounts Committee the previous year.

To close out this round and in response to MacLean's probing on the Premier's interventions on lease negotiations, the tender for the Municipal Affairs space was brought up. This was the first major lease to follow the new public tender policy.

Ralph Medjuck, the Premier's friend, and former law partner was not the low bidder, and I was directed by the Premier to allow him to submit an alternate proposal. The other bidders were given the same opportunity and the second-round results did not improve Medjuck's ranking.

I was called over to the Premier's office with Terry Donahoe to review the spreadsheet of the bid results, and the Premier said to me 'Michael the Minister of the Department wants to move, and you know my wishes I would like very much to see this go to Mr. Medjuck. I will accept your recommendations whatever it is, and we will live with that.'

I went back to my office and to protect the integrity of the new public tender policy, awarded the lease contract to the low bidder. Within two weeks I was on my way to a government facilitated psychiatric assessment.

Moody kicked off the second round of questioning for the government side and this time the gloves were off, and he was out for blood.

MR. MOODY: Mr. Zareski you indicated you had some discussions with Mr. MacEachern. Were these meetings prior to this meeting today to go over lines of questioning for you, and did you have discussions on different things that were your views when you were Deputy Minister of Government Services?

MR. ZARESKI: Quite frankly, Mr. Moody there was a suggestion that it might be appropriate to meet him but I would not meet with anybody prior to coming to this hearing today. I stayed out of communication for a week prior to coming to this committee meeting.

MR. MOODY: Prior to the week you say?

MR. ZARESKI: I said for the week prior.

MR. MOODY: The week prior but there were discussions before that.

MR. ZARESKI: No, they were not. Not with respect to the questioning of this committee, no.

MR. MOODY: Okay, but there were discussions about a number of things. You indicated that you were rushed out of government in a couple of weeks. I know that not to be true, I know that there was a lot of feeling to assist you during your difficulties and have you remained in government,

I fail to understand. When you were having your difficulties and you left, without indicating to anyone where you were and that sort of thing, is that a normal practice for any deputy minister or anybody in a responsible position?

MR. ZARESKI: Mr. Moody I was on vacation, and I had called my secretary to tell her that I was going to take an extra week and I would be back early the following week. At that time, I asked her to appoint Mr. Hiltz as the acting deputy minister so I did inform my employer as to the fact that I was not going to be there. The relationship that I had with my ex-wife is my private and personal matter.

MR. MOODY: I'm not talking about that; I'm talking about the relationship with government. At what point did you stop going to your office, did anyone keep you from going to your office? Why did you not return to your office?

MR. ZARESKI: Because my integrity was taken away from me. The government questioned my mental competency my effectiveness and my ability to do my job and I could not function under those circumstances, and I did not know if they would do similar things again Mr. Moody.

MR. MOODY: Do you think that if your integrity was questioned, it might have been related to your actions?

MR. ZARESKI: If there was a question within my actions, then why didn't the government discuss my actions before they took the action that they took? I had no communication, no knowledge of any plans, or any concern that the government had with respect to my functioning as a deputy minister. In fact, as I recall watching a news program on which the interview was done by Mr. Grant of ATV news, Terry Donahue made very exemplary comments about my performance as a deputy minister.

MR. MOODY: Yes, I thought so when I was there too. Did you feel that you had special power, that you were unique in any way when you were going through this difficulty?

MR. ZARESKI: No, the only thing that I have Mr. Moody is my honesty and my integrity and my desire to do the right thing and if that is the special power, God bless me.

The questioning continued with Marie Dechman from the government side suggested that I was at the Public Accounts hearing with a personal vendetta and asked if I had any litigation before the courts at this moment in relationship to suing the government for any kind of damages to which I replied 'Not as yet'

She then directed her remarks to the Chairman citing the sub judice convention in the House of Assembly she expressed the concern that a witness coming before the committee with the intent of suing the provincial government and the line of questioning that is going on could influence the court's decision with evidence from the committee. She felt it was not good for practice for the Public Accounts Committee to bring in witnesses for when there is a court case pending.

Vince MacLean then spoke up on a point of order saying that what Mr. Zareski intends to do in the future is up to him and at the moment there is dealing with a situation where there's no litigation and therefore the sub judice rule would not apply.

Here I must give credit to the government's information network. I had in fact been in contact with Howard Levitt an employment lawyer from Toronto to review my situation and give his input on the likelihood of succeeding with a constructive dismissal case. He was prepared to consider taking my case on a pro bono basis however following further discussion it appeared to me that his motivation was more for his reputation then it was for seeking justice on my behalf and as we did not come to agreement on the terms on his engagement, the discussions went no further.

Mrs. Dechman then taking up the baton handed to her by George Moody was incredulous that John MacEachern would come along out of the blue to befriend and want to help. By way of explanation, she was informed that I was living in his constituency and that he was calling me in his role as the Liberal Justice Critic. At the time, he was aware of the reports in the newspapers and on radio about my relationship with government and how it was severed. He indicated that he was calling the Attorney General's Department to try to find out information about the circumstances and every time he called, he got stonewalled. They would not give him any information where previously to that they were very helpful in keeping him informed as to the cases that they were working on, or the relationships that they had in similar circumstances.

He reached out to me in a very forward and honest way to find out the facts for himself. Mr. MacEachern offered to make inquiries on my behalf to see what was going on. I told her that I had no communication from anybody else in the government except Terry Donahue who visited me in the Abbie Lane Hospital and with whom I met in Sydney after leaving Homewood.

After continued persistent questioning I reiterated several times that there were no discussions with anyone inside or outside of government with respect to the upcoming committee hearing. I only found out that I would be called as a witness two weeks before the hearing date and I did not know what the line of questioning would be. I am here to give you and the rest of the committee the facts as I know them.

With Mrs. Deckman's time expired, the same line of questioning was resumed by David Nantes.

MR. NANTES: When you left government in June 1989, did you discuss it with any elected member of government, either before you left or after you left, until Mr. Donahoe who contacted you?

MR: ZARESKI: Before I left government, I had indicated to Mr. Donahoe that I was going to be leaving the government eventually. I could not see myself being a deputy minister for the next twenty-five years. I felt that I had other things that I wanted to pursue and I was too young to stay in that kind of work for the rest of my working career. I was quite frank with him that I was going to keep my eyes open for other opportunities.

MR. NANTES: When you left your office in June 1989, you said you were taking a weeks' vacation, or something like that. Is it true that you made no contact with the government until Mr. Donahue was able to locate you in Cape Breton in August and he called you and asked you to meet with him? Is that the first contact you made with any of your employers?

MR. ZARESKI: That is not true.

MR. NANTES: Well, what is true?

MR. ZARESKI: What is true is that I spoke to the government on the following Monday to my secretary.

MR. NANTES: No, no. I asked about elected officials. Who…

MR. ZARESKI: Mr. Donahoe met me at the Abbie Lane Hospital prior to me going away and I have a letter from you (as Minister of Health), another contact, indicating that all my expenses would be paid. The government certainly knew I was in the Homewood, so I certainly did not have to call the government to tell them where I was.

MR. NANTES: How long did you stay in the Homewood Center?

MR. ZARESKI: I was there until July the 7th.

MR. NANTES: How long did you stay?

MR. ZARESKI: From June 18th or 20th to July the 7th whatever that works out to be.

MR. NANTES: Did you leave with a doctor's permission, or did you decide yourself to leave?

MR. ZARESKI: While I was there, the doctors could not find anything wrong with me; there was no treatment prescribed to me; I was given full freedom of the grounds and of the city of Guelph Ontario and I agreed to stay until every test that they had for me was completed.

MR. NANTES: Would you agree, Mr. Zareski, that the doctors did not want you to leave?

MR. ZARESKI: The doctors did not say that they did not want me to leave, I would not agree with that.

MR. NANTES: You would not agree with that.

MR. ZARESKI: I know that.

MR. NANTES: You felt that you left after the doctors felt that they had done their full treatment?

MR. ZARESKI: Exactly, I have their medical records to substantiate this.

MR. NANTES: That is very interesting because the medical reports, as you know, government sometimes seeks assurances when it's sending someone out-of-province, that they go out-of-province to seek a treatment that is not available in Nova Scotia.

The report back to government, I believe, or at least the indication back to government was that you left, really, without them agreeing.

Mr. MacLean interrupted, claiming that for the Minister of Health to use privileged information is totally inappropriate.

Nantes then started back peddling when he realized the mistake that he had made. He had put his foot in his mouth and would end up choking on it.

MR. NANTES: Mr. Chairman, on the point of order I would like to make it very clear that I had no confidential information, but I think it would be fair to say that family members of Mr. Zareski were aware that Mr. Zareski left without a doctor's agreement. I have no confidential information; I have no written reports from doctors, other than the information that came from very concerned family members.

Notwithstanding the fact that my testimony clearly stated that I was in Homewood for an assessment and have the records to prove that there is nothing wrong with me, the common narrative consistently emphasized by my ex-wife, certain family members, Dr. Teehan and the government was that I had been sent away for treatment and had left without permission. This was clearly the narrative that they wanted the public to believe.

By Dr. Ferguson agreeing to inform my family that I would be leaving Homewood a few days after my discharge, confirmed to me that he was suspicious of the motives of my family and employer. The only family member with permission to receive information about my stay was my brother David who obviously was David Nantes' source. This was more verification that there was a conspiracy to get me out of the picture and that the plan had been in the works for some time.

For all intents and purposes, the Public Accounts Committee hearing was over. A political bomb had been dropped on the Buchanan government painting a picture of institutionalized patronage masterminded by Premier Buchanan and the damage that afternoon was irreparable. The battle lines had been drawn, and with the opening volley fired the war had just begun.

CHAPTER 9

Innuendos Intensify

O utside the hearing room the media scrum pounced for comments with one reporter suggesting that because my testimony was protected by parliamentary privilege I could get away with the revelations without fear of legal reprisal. The least of my concerns was legal reprisal if it was a concern at all. After all, I've lost my family; my friends, my home; my career, what more can they take away from me?

Outside the protection of the Public Accounts Committee, I shot back revealing Buchanan personally benefited by having his Leiblin Drive home painted and repairs done to his Piggot Lake summer cottage by government employees; and that the mail messenger staff served as chauffeurs and ran personal errands for the Buchanan family.

The government tried to paint me as either a mentally ill unfortunate or a vengeful saboteur, while the opposition hailed me as an honorable man who has blown the lid of a corrupt system of patronage, payoffs, and crooked deals.

"The testimony presented some of the most damning statements and scenarios that I have ever heard in the sixteen years that I have been a member of the house." said Vince MacLean. "This is a top man in the government showing that he's been involved in the awarding of tenders and contracts and it's just the biggest scandal that has hit the legislature, and it will bring a stain on politics and unfortunate national attention to Nova Scotia. The public will feel that all politicians are the same."

Both opposition leaders Vince MacLean and Alexa McDonough were quick to call for a full RCMP investigation into the allegations.

MacLean also called for the resignation of David Nantes as Minister of Health for breaching confidentiality by releasing medical information in an underhanded, sleazy, and totally inappropriate way. It was clearly reprehensible to reinforce the unfair stereotype that an individual who sees a psychiatrist must be mentally unstable.

Nantes denied that he had released any confidential information about my mental health and rejected the call that he should resign. He argued that as the minister he simply signed a document that authorized me to go out-of-province for treatment and that it was the compassionate way to deal with the situation.

This fabricated need for treatment was based on trumped up accusations which suited the government's narrative without a full mental health assessment having been carried out. The collaborators in this scheme erred in sending me out of the province and lost control of their plan which eventually backfired.

The Conservative government painted me as a bright civil servant who developed psychiatric problems when his marriage broke up. The premier and other ministers under fire by my allegations defended themselves by continuing to describe me as mentally incompetent.

By the end of the week, the press either found or perhaps given my discharge summary from Homewood, on file under seal in the public court records dealing with my divorce. The document affirmed my testimony at Public Accounts that psychiatrists at the Homewood last year found nothing wrong with me that marital problems and a midlife crisis didn't explain. The document confirmed my squeaky-clean bill of physical and mental health and dispelled the innuendo alluded to by government officials about my emotional stability.

After a long day of intense meeting with senior advisors a press conference was called for Buchanan to defend himself. He unequivocally wanted to assure Nova Scotians that there was no truth in statements made against his character at public accounts and during the last number of days.

He told a packed news conference that the statements have caused a great deal of anguish to himself and his family. He denied receiving any kickbacks and said no government funds were spent painting his house or repairing his cottage. He said it was fine with him that the RCMP were looking into the matter and admitted that his government had been damaged by the allegations.

He continued his attack on me as being mentally unstable and therefore not credible saying there was not a shred of truth in anything that I said. He railed against me for my accusations and later said "Something happened to him early last year before leaving the job." When pressed by a reporter for more detail all he would say was "I have suspicions, that that's all. I have information that was given to me, but I told you, I'm not going to discuss that. That's something that I don't think is proper for me to discuss."

His assertion that my performance had suffered since early 1989 contradicts statements made by my immediate boss Terry Donahue who had said that my performance in government was exemplary and by the Attorney General Tom McInnis who publicly stated that I had done nothing wrong during my five years as a deputy minister.

He didn't know what to say when a reporter told him she had seen the medical reports from Homewood showing me to be normal. Buchanan declined to comment saying" I'm not a psychiatrist, I haven't seen the reports, and I'm not going to comment on psychiatric reports." But that didn't stop his earlier statements impugning my character and integrity through his false comments and innuendo suggesting psychological problems were behind the allegations.

The Premier then in desperation to divert attention from himself, focused his attack on the Liberals claiming that the allegations were part of a Liberal plot to discredit and destroy his government and suggested that the leading questions by the Liberals at Public Accounts were rehearsed with me prior to my appearance.

The opposition parties continued to reinforce the point that efforts to undermine my credibility with suggestions about my mental health was part of a smear campaign in an orchestrated response by the government to try to undermine probably the person who has given the most damning information on the internal workings of the Buchanan government by spreading rumors of the most vicious kind.

MacLean and McDonough said they didn't need the clinic's discharge report to be convinced of my credibility. My demeanor intelligence and what was said at the public accounts did the job. The NDP leader confirmed that not one single phone call disputing my testimony, or my credibility was received. At the liberal offices MacLean said the public has not questioned my integrity or intelligence or competence and he found that quite interesting.

McDonough predicted the government will not be able to contain the damage from the revelations. It's totally unstoppable in the sense that the Tory government is gone! MacLean suggests my testimony has undermined the moral integrity of the government, and that it is going to have difficulty functioning. He said the discharge summary report will only serve to give more credibility to the rest of my allegations and he quite rightly suspected there was more to come.

Rather than dealing with the allegations of questionable government contracts and payments levelled in the House of Assembly question period, Donahoe attacked my mental competence by saying, "We are dealing with discussion and dialogue and testimony in front of committees which has the potential to further seriously and adversely affecting the rest of the life of a very promising young forty-year-old."

Donahoe denied my version of the hiring a Rocca Construction; of the discussion about Don Powers contract; about the hiring of Lloyd McQueen; and that government employees painted the Premier's house. In parliamentary terms he was calling me a liar.

Vince MacLean said in Question Period that "Zareski had been a model employee until he told the truth. The government wants to make sure he was smeared publicly to undermine his allegations and has set out single mindedly to destroy his credibility."

My testimony was accepted by the opposition side because it substantiated many concerns and suspicions held about the systemic patronage of the Buchanan government. The real question of course is whether there will be enough hard evidence to make the allegations stick.

Events were moving fast and furious. The gloves came off with a renewed attack which failed miserably when my clean bill of health was found by the media. My concern now was that the government may launch a different kind of attack.

I knew that my every move was being watched and that my phone calls were tapped as evidenced by the clicking sound on the line. There was a lot at stake for certain members of government and those who supported them if my testimony could not be muzzled. I knew these individuals from working with them and seeing how they work behind the scenes, and they can be vicious.

A lot of people stood to lose positions of power and authority if they are unsuccessful in discrediting me. An accident could be arranged, or I could have easily been suicided with the narrative being the poor man the stress of what he went through was too much for him to handle.

I then decided it was time to publicly express these concerns in a way that would bring attention to them and mitigate attempts by my adversaries to do something stupid. In an interview I told the media that I was being cautious about where I went and said if anything happened to me, carry out an investigation.

CHAPTER 10

Cover Up in the Works

The RCMP who had been reviewing the Public Accounts Committee transcripts to determine if there was sufficient evidence to launch a criminal investigation called to set up a meeting with me in Sydney. We met for a couple of hours and it was my view that most of the allegations had less to do with criminality and more to do with Buchanan's patronage and corruption activities, many of which were thwarted before they could take effect.

For example, Medjuck was not awarded the lease for Municipal Affairs; the $30,000 payment to Cleary to give up the Canstone shares was not made; The Rehab Hospital was awarded to the low bidder Lundrigan's, not Buchanan's pick Corkum Construction.

The more contentious allegations with possible criminal overtones related to work done on Buchanan's home and cottage and a new topic I brought up related to the anonymous call about drug dealing by a mail messenger in the Provincial Building stairwell which elicited a series of questions from the RCMP.

Did I know that the provincial government bought all of the pharmaceutical drugs for the provincial hospitals through the Central Pharmacy at the Nova Scotia Hospital; that the list of companies that these drugs were bought from was reviewed and approved by the Premier; that Norm Atkinson ex-RCMP and holding a senior position in Government Services as Director of Security for the province coordinated this activity;

that stale-dated drugs were not returned or destroyed, and that volume discounts for drug purchases did not go back against the contract but went directly to Buchanan?

I had to admit that as Deputy I did not know any of this and it put in perspective the extent of the trafficking going on within government circles masterminded by Buchanan. It also made a link to the toilet seat caper as to why the government would be dealing with the Cranston brothers' known drug dealers and having 200 seats delivered to the top floor of the Provincial Building

Were the boxes that contained the toilet seats used as the method for bringing drugs in for distribution? Why was the information about the drugs brought to my attention, when it was not part of the Public Accounts testimony? Was Atkinson an informer for the RCMP or was he under investigation as well? From this and other information shared with the RCMP I was convinced that they had more than enough to lay criminal charges.

That did not stop me from using this information about the pharmaceutical drugs as if it were my own. A day or so later I was speaking to a senior reporter at CBC and shared what was divulged to me by the RCMP. Within a couple of days that reporter was transferred to Toronto to join the National Business Desk. The story was obviously too hot to handle.

A week or so later I received a call from a CBC reporter from Sydney looking for a scoop. I told him the same story and he said to me 'Mr. Zareski you can't expect me to believe this. This is preposterous.' I suggested he conduct his own investigation.

A few days later he called back saying everything that I had told him he found to be true and more. He mentioned not only Buchanan's involvement but Donahoe's as well and indicated that an expose would be on Thursday night's supper hour news. Thursday night came and went and there was no expose.

Two weeks later I bumped into the reporter on the sidewalk on Spring Garden Rd. in Halifax and asked him what happened to the story. He informed me he no longer works for the CBC and was going to be moving to the United States the next day. That was the end of it, the story died there and has not been repeated by me until now.

Following the RCMP interview a press conference was held announcing that a criminal investigation would be launched into the allegations raised at the Public Accounts Committee against the Government.

The federal police force said in their news release that the investigation will be directed at some aspects of several allegations related to procedures at the Government Services Department. Although my allegations focused almost exclusively on the activities of the Premier he was not named as the subject of the investigation; a point used by Buchanan when asked by reporters if he would be stepping down.

The vague wording of the focus of the RCMP investigation which eliminated reference to any of the participants in the patronage practices was deliberately done to limit the scope of their probe...a cover up was in the works.

Almost immediately there was a loud and clear message coming from the NDP and several newspaper editorials pushing for a full public inquiry. The Liberals for their part skirted around the periphery shifting the focus away from the patronage and corruption allegations and zeroing in on the call for David Nantes resignation for improperly disclosing personal medical information thereby missing completely the broader matter of public interest in the charges.

The Liberals remained leery up until now of my unsubstantiated charges and their performance in the last week of the sitting of the legislature was described as surprisingly gutless and unimaginative. At the very least, while the controversy was fresh, they had a responsibility to fulfill their parliamentary role with vigor and courage by ensuring that the idea of a public inquiry into patronage was firmly planted in the public mind.

Unless I was completely discredited as a witness, I was potentially the key to a devastating assault on the Nova Scotia patronage system which could lead to permanent and substantive reforms and perhaps this is why both the Liberals and Conservatives were so afraid of pursuing it.

The announcement of the criminal investigation was a blow to Buchanan. When besieged by reporters asking if he had any intentions of stepping down, he defended himself saying no, he would not step down because his name wasn't mentioned in the RCMP statement.

Buchanan appeared weary and dejected; the man who once campaigned on the slogan 'Honest it's John for Nova Scotia', and who carried the nickname 'Teflon John' for avoiding association with the past political scandals of his ministers was now, for the first time, directly in the spotlight. The current allegations are potentially most damaging because they are directly linked to the Premier.

Buchanan expressed that "It is a bit traumatic to go through this kind of nonsense." Replying to a question, he went on to admit that he found the last few days particularly upsetting, "Well, certainly, why wouldn't I? Someone making false nonsense and accusations like that."

He admonished the media to "Go out and find the real facts on this. Do some checking about the gentleman who made the statements, I just feel sorry for him. I feel betrayed by someone I tried to help."

As evidenced by the response to a Hotline call in, the public sentiment was overwhelmingly against Buchanan and his government. Hotliners from across Nova Scotia declared that the electorate should run the government out of the province on a rail.

To the questions asked "Do the charges of government corruption and allegation kickbacks involving Premium Buchanan confirm with your view of his government? Or is the author of these charges conducting a smear campaign? A record response with almost 80% of the sample confirmed the suspicions of corruption in the Buchanan government.

Buchanan did have his supporters with one caller saying that I was put up to the whole thing by the sleazy liberals and another saying that the idea that you would consider giving the likes of Michael Zareski more credibility than our Premier's able government is morally reprehensible.

However, the sentiment expressing shame on those who cast aspersions on a person's character and intellect by referring to a past mental issue, real or fictional, was well represented by the callers.

CHAPTER 11

Significant Turn of Events

T
he calls for David Nantes' resignation were unrelenting. John MacEachern had in a letter earlier that year to the Health Minister on January 12th asked if the government was financing my treatment in an out-of-province facility and on what authority.

Nantes had replied that the information requested was confidential and personal and therefore cannot be released under the Freedom of Information Act and the Health Services and Insurance Act. To which MacEachern replied that the Minister either didn't tell the truth about not being able to share confidential information regarding payment and authority for confinement, or he was telling the truth, and was now breaching confidentiality. If the Minister wants to try again to say that he has never had any confidential information, he will have to face the new accusation that his questions in Public Accounts were driven by the single purpose of discrediting me and should resign.

Dr. Jim Smith the Liberal health critic said, "Nantes has done more in a single day to destroy all the good that's been done on mental health in the last decade in Nova Scotia and that minister should resign." Smith then requested an emergency debate which was turned down.

There was an understanding from the opposition that David Nantes would step aside while authorities decided whether to charge him. The rumors circulating that Nantes had offered his resignation to Buchanan had been denied by Nantes at first but later in the same interview he was evasive saying "I will not attempt to even answer that question, so you are not getting an indication of yes or no, or even if I have offered such a thing." Nantes then refused to answer a dozen or so more questions. Appearing somewhat shaken, he gave a similar reply each time. "I gave all my comments last week and I have no additional comments to make."

Buchanan, true to form defending Nantes saying that he's done nothing illegal and released no confidential information whatsoever. He denied that Nantes' credibility is in question or that there was a cloud of suspicion over Nantes' head other than the one placed by the opposition. Buchanan chalked it all up to politics. In Buchanan's world view morally reprehensible activities are not a problem if one is not caught or charged with an offense.

Whether or not they believe the Public Account allegations, many Nova Scotians were generally distressed and deeply offended by David Nantes' attempt to discredit me by alluding to my stay in a psychiatric hospital. It offended elementary fairness and common decency to hear the province's chief health official drag personal medical information into a political fight which should be settled on the truth of or inaccuracy of the allegations The public looking at the bigger picture, saw the Nantes' question primarily as a matter of ethics not one of law.

In that sense it didn't really matter whether the remarks were made under privilege or on the street or whether the information came from a file, or from family. The minister had a duty to use absolute restraint in discussing the personal health of individuals without their consent regardless of the source of the information. The prevailing public opinion was that by acting in a way that implies someone who consults a psychiatrist is thereby unstable and unreliable Mr. Nantes conduct has been incompatible with his duties and responsibilities as Minister of Health and whatever the outcome of the legal investigation, the proper course of action was for him to step down.

If Nantes tendered his resignation, it would have been political suicide for the Premier to accept it. By doing so, the first chink in the armor exposing the governments vulnerability and leading to its collapse would be in place, and all would go downhill after that.

Meanwhile Attorney General Tom McInnis, who claimed all along that it was not up to him to investigate Nantes, forwarded the Public

Accounts transcript to the Halifax City police to decide if charges will be laid against the minister.

Days later, following their executive meeting the president Nova Scotia Medical Society said that the issue of confidentiality is a basic premise in the practice of medicine and if the minister has in fact broken confidentiality there needs to be a public investigation. The medical society would not be involved in that investigation because the matter had been referred to the Halifax Police Department and therefore it was now a legal matter.

The timing of the police investigation could not have worked out better for the medical society who a year ago refused to investigate the doctors who collaborated with the minister to send me away for an assessment that was not called for; they were able to duck the issue a second time.

The request to have the Halifax Police Department carry out the Nantes' investigation became a political hot potato with the city questioning who should bear the cost and claiming it was a major political matter belonging to the RCMP, not the city police.

The Attorney General's weak excuse was that the incident, which occurred at the Provincial Legislature, fell within city jurisdiction. When asked, the Chief of Police said that this is the first time 'in a long time' that the police department has been asked to investigate a case involving an incident at the Legislature.

The Halifax police dithered with the investigation for a month then announced their political decision not to charge Nantes with a summary offence because Nantes' remarks were protected by parliamentary privilege. The police admitted they did not consider subsequent statements made by the health minister outside the legislature because the correspondence from the Attorney General's office was interpreted as a complaint about what Nantes said during Public Accounts and they had received no complaint about anything that was said outside the actual meeting.

The police probe left a lot of unanswered questions and caused a bit of furor amongst the opposition members who rejected the police findings and renewed the call for Nantes' resignation. The public, for their part, questioned the thoroughness of the sloppy investigation by the police who seemed to be the laughingstock of town.

In their reporting of the police decision, CBC broadcast the videotape of Mr. Nantes' comments to members of the media outside the committee room, and with this new information the police agreed to further review the circumstances surrounding all of the statements made by the minister. The on again, off again, police investigation was now on again.

The Halifax police officers questioned all media and "non-media persons" present at the June 13th scrum and followed up with letters to all media agencies requesting their videotapes. None were willing to comply unless the police produced a search warrant. A month later, with warrant in hand at least ten officers spent two hours wading through hundreds of CBC television tapes before the corporation staff on legal advice relinquished the unedited field tape.

The CBC were reluctant to hand over the tapes for number of reasons, including the feeling that police had other means to attain a full account of the exchange and that relinquishing the unedited field tape would be looked upon as handing over a reporter's notebook.

In short order the police found what they were looking for and charged Health Minister David Nantes with two counts - one charge under the Freedom of Information Act and the other under the Health Services and Insurance Act with the arraignment to appear in Provincial Court on 10 October.

The not so well thought out strategy of the government to release my confidential medical information to discredit my allegations backfired. As a result, David Nantes had no choice but to resign from cabinet.

CHAPTER 12

Drip - Drip - Drip

The beleaguered Conservative government remained powerless to mount any effective counter offense. The strategy of dropping the bombshells at the Public Accounts Committee followed up by the Chinese torture phase of releasing additional bits of information drip by drip seemed to be working.

My plan all along was to release information in stages; giving too much all at once would be too much for the public to absorb. For the plan to work, it was important to oblige the journalists' calls with courtesy, careful not to thrust myself forward, thereby gaining a measure of trust and respect. By assuming a passive attitude to the whole affair, while holding a bottomless pit of tantalizing information on the inner workings of the government, the media called constantly, hungry for more.

The less spectacular contents of the follow-up news provided no comfort for the Conservatives, for whom the constant drip, drip, drip of patronage allegations and their weak denials continued to have a politically corrosive effect. People did not tune out completely with the story playing out in the background with periodical minders that the government remained under a cloud of unrefuted allegations.

A secondary effect was that many people accepted the general tenor of the indictments that shone a light on Nova Scotia's blatant old boy patronage style of politics This could be a death blow for that style, and lead to effective and real reform in the practice of government and the political culture of the province. Only time will tell.

By mid-July it appeared that interest was waning, the mid-summer political news doldrums were kicking in and it was time to turn up the heat a notch and provide fresh allegations for the media to dig into.

In response to one of the frequent 'what's up' calls, I passed on the information about the government paying $50,000 for 200 electric toilet seats, which featured a motor and storage compartment holding a roll of plastic sleeves which were dispensed at the press of a button. Explicit instructions to purchase the seats from the Premier's friend Bobby Cranston came directly from Buchanan's office. The seats ended up in a government warehouse and were never used.

The media were on the trail of the sensational story and although significant information was unearthed it was just as quickly buried and not following up. Initially Terry Donahue as Minister of Government Services claimed ultimate responsibility for purchasing the seats. However, he was not the minister in 1988 when the order was placed – perhaps he was running cover to take the heat off of Buchanan.

Donahoe went on to tell reporters that after the seats were received the plan to distribute them was put on hold by the Health Department because they would heighten public fears that AIDS could be contracted from them. His justification for buying the seats at an exorbitant price because they were a high-tech unique product didn't hold water.

The story was flushed out days later when Donahoe admitted to a meeting in 1988 while he was Attorney General with paroled drug dealer Murdoch Cranston and his brother Robert, both of whom worked for Rodco Distributers after it was taken over the same year by Alex Stephen, to discuss the purchase of high-tech total seats.

Murdock convicted in 1984 of possessing 22 kilograms of hashish for the purpose of trafficking was on parole for an 8-year sentence while Rodco's owner Alex Stephen had a criminal record for attempting to import morphine into Canada and was sentenced in 1983 to 20 years in prison.

Following his parole, Cranston was also paid $30,000 by his friend Yarmouth developer John Miller to lobby Donahoe and Buchanan his longtime friends to lease the historic but now derelict and vacant Morses

Tea warehouse building across from Privateers Wharf in downtown Halifax at current office space prices.

Donahoe bristled when a reporter asked if he had reservations about dealing with people with drug records. Clearly, by his answer, it didn't bother him one bit. "I guess I want to wonder whether by putting that the question, you asked whether someone on parole isn't allowed to have a life and to attempt a business and to live in the community." he replied. "I don't know whether that thought ever crossed my mind, I was looking at a product." I wondered what the product really was that he was looking at, because it certainly wasn't the toilet seats.

Ask why the Cranston's would approach him when he was Attorney General Donahoe said. "Because they know me, I know them they're here all the time." "I see them around, I speak to them on occasion, and they speak to me I've seen them for 25 years around the streets of Halifax, here at Province House, all over."

The next day Donahoe acknowledged again that he met with the brothers but said he couldn't remember if he lobbied on their behalf. The Premier also admitted knowing the Cranston's and agreed with a reporter's description of Bobby Cranston as a friend. However, he said he hasn't heard from Murdock in "umpteen years".

Did Donahoe who admits being friends with the Cranston's for 25 years or more know of their involvement with drug trafficking over that time? The question remains, why would drug dealers, convicted or not, have such a close relationship to both Donahue and Buchanan? The Cranton brothers both constituents of Buchanan's Spryfield riding had a reputation for selling drugs a lot longer than selling toilet seats.

If Donahue doesn't recall lobbying on behalf of the Cranston's, then why did he meet with them in the first place? What was the path of the ultimatum to buy the seats - where did it come from? Was it a request from Cranston to Donahue that then went to Buchanan that resulted in the order to me from the Premier's Press Secretary John O'Brien to buy the seats? Or did it start with the Premier giving instructions to Donahoe to meet with the Cranston's and comeback with a plan? Were the seats the product that was being bought or were they simply a vehicle for the delivery of a product to be resold? Where and when were the seats initially delivered and who received them? These were the dots that the press did not follow up on and if those connections were made the implications for both Buchanan and Donahoe would have been serious.

By early August, remarks made by Buchanan gave the impression that he had thrown in the towel and already walked away from the job. In a fifty-minute talk with reporters he came across as dispirited and cynical while his government was crumbling around him. At one point, he said he could defend against the patronage allegations, but doubted the media would use his evidence and when asked why he wouldn't answer questions about his connections with lobbyists and convicted drug dealer Murdock Cranston he questioned his own credibility saying he didn't know if people would believe him.

When reporters asked why he has not provided proof to counter the allegations, the Premier said the proof is in government files, but he wasn't convinced he should take the logical step of sitting down with reporters to answer their question. The real problem was that information contained in government files supported the allegations and after a month and a half there was nothing found to refute them.

It was an odd situation to have the Premier under pressure by the media to defend himself, question his own credibility. It was especially uncharacteristic for Buchanan, a seasoned politician noted for his gift of blarney and effusive boisterousness to express such self-doubt at a news conference.

Up until now, there has been a measure of forbearance by the public and media to the allegations of personal corruption by the Premier, who now offends those who would give him the benefit of the doubt by suggesting that he has already been lynched.

In the end, with the admission that the government has been under pressure to respond to the allegations and that the public certainly had a right to know, Buchanan promised in the next few days to get various ministers to release fact sheets with more information to refute the allegations.

But Terry Donahoe, whose department is the chief one involved, refuse to go along with the idea saying it would be inappropriate at this time to be going around shooting off his mouth while the matter is under investigation.

It appeared that the long knives were coming out. Buchanan would not be supported by his ministers in coming forward with the long-promised fact sheets. Buchanan's cabinet ministers had abandoned the Premier to the wolves and were not doing anything to defend their boss.

Two weeks later reporters still looking for the fact sheets were told by the Premier, "Look just bide your time - you'll get some information; give me a little breathing space will you please. They will be produced within the month."

Eventually Buchanan provided receipts and cancelled cheques for work done on the cottage in 1983 when Don Power was the Deputy Minister. The documents included statements from the men that they did the work entirely on evenings and weekends and days off and that they transported themselves to and from the cottage by private vehicle and that they were paid in full by personal cheque. One of the workers who signed the statement for the Premier said he drew up his statement when his foreman asked him to do so.

Digging into the photocopies of the receipts provided by various suppliers, reporters found that the companies who provided the copies would not allow reporters to view the originals. One company went so far as to use a current receipt number which they backdated to 1983 because they said the original was too faded.

The information on the cottage repairs submitted by Buchanan did not refute the allegations made outside of Public Account which were subsequently corroborated by a former Government Services employee interviewed as part of the RCMP investigation.

The former employee said the whole side of the Piggot Lake cottage was repaired with lumber, stain, and nails bought with government purchase orders He said that on several occasions in 1984, he delivered the materials along with government tradesmen to the cottage in a government truck during working hours under orders from his superior - knowing that it was wrong but doing what he was told, saying that "It was so common place that he didn't really thing about it."

While the RCMP was going through the motions of an investigation to keep the public and opposition parties satisfied and the media at bay, the internal evidence that was being gathered to indicate criminality on Buchanan's part was growing, especially the drug connection.

The information on the distribution network for pharmaceutical drugs and the Cranston brother's connection with the Premier was information now known by both the RCMP and the CBC. There is no doubt that the top brass in both organizations were also aware and by extension, so was the Prime Minister's office. Brian Mulrooney, a close political ally and personnel friend of Buchanan had to have been kept informed of events as they unfolded.

If an intrepid reporter were able to uncover what was really going on, the Public Accounts allegations on corruption and political patronage would be nothing more than a 'tempest in a teapot' compared to the catastrophic political storm that would ensue if Buchanan's drug dealing enterprise ever leaked out.

A political diversion was needed to draw the attention from the RCMP investigation and the scanty support the Premier was getting from his colleagues who were letting him fend for himself. The problem was conveniently resolved on September 13th with the Premier's resignation which was followed on the same afternoon by his appointment to the Senate by Brian Mulroney.

The two men cut from the same political cloth were if nothing else extremely loyal to each other. Buchanan often acted as Mulrooney's lapdog, holding his tongue when federal policies were at odds with those of the Provinces. Now one of Buchanan top duties as a Senator will be to help speed up the passage of the controversial goods and services sales tax which he opposed for years. His loyalty to Mulrooney was apparent when Buchanan admitted that although he still opposes the tax, he won't be voting against it.

"Last spring my family and I decided that after 24 years in the legislature, 20 years as party leader and 12 years as Premier that I would retire in late 1990 or January 1991" Buchanan said in a written statement. "My decision to accept the Senate appointment just advances that date by several months." Buchanan went on to respond to a reporter's question saying "My decision has nothing whatsoever to do with the recent scandals.

The resignation of Premier John Buchanan might have caught everyone off guard, but I was not surprised. Buchanan was getting out before he was given the boot. An extremely astute politician with a keen sense of history, he wouldn't want to be the only Premier of this province kicked out of office in disgrace. Buchanan felt his downfall was inevitable – that is why he accepted the senate position - Buchanan has admitted defeat.

Mulrooney brushed off opposition to the appointment of scandal plagued Buchanan saying the former Premier is innocent until proven guilty.

The Premier's departure was extremely well timed. Not only was the blatant patronage politically expedient for both men, but it made the Senate look like a handy escape hatch for politicians in trouble. There must have been an awful lot of negotiations going on over the last number of weeks to get him that senate job – it's just another kind of patronage - only at a higher level.

Buchanan was never a fan of the Senate and had previously called for the institution to be abolished arguing that "As a house of second thought it really didn't fill that bill because it was not responsible to the people." His criticism was further voiced in June of this year when he was quoted as saying, "In the last number of years it has really not been a meaningful institution in this country." And two and a half months prior to the appointment Buchanan was asked if he would consider a senate seat if one were offered him was on record saying, "Let's put it this way: there is no senate seat that is challenging enough for me."

The appointment sparked outrage on editorial pages across the country and flooded government offices with calls of protest with public comment more hostile in tone than any similar move on the seedy history of patronage. One editorial said that "The appointment would have been acceptable, even laudable, if Mulrooney waited for the RCMP investigation to be concluded. It is absolutely bewildering why the Prime Minister would appoint Buchanan now and equally bewildering why Buchanan would accept the invitation. " If truth be known, there was no choice in the matter, the appointment had to be made when it was to keep the lid on Buchanan's criminal activities.

Parker Barss Donham, a prominent free-lance CBC personality working out of Cape Breton showed up with his camera crew at my residence in Cape Breton looking for an interview on my thoughts about the departure. While his crew was setting up, Parker took me aside and told me that the VP for News and Public Affairs from CBC headquarters had given him instructions to make me look bad. So much for the independence of media, especially the publicly funded version. Needless to say, thanks to Mr. Donham the interview went well.

After 12 years in office the cost of Buchanan's stewardship was crippling to Nova Scotians. On taking over the government in 1978, the provincial debt was $500 million with a budget of $1.2 billion. On his departure the debt was approaching $5 billion with an annual budget that topped $4 billion, this accumulation of debt resulted in an ever-increasing portion of the provincial budget allocated to debt payment which almost doubled from eleven cents to twenty cents on the dollar resulting in a two-point drop in the province credit rating.

In addition, the unaccountable politically controlled Crown corporations, boards, and agencies under Buchanan's stewardship racked up an additional $2.6 billion in contingent liabilities. The banksters did well for themselves during the Buchanan era and set up the way forward to take an ever-increasing share of taxpayer's income.

It was no surprise that after a 14-month RCMP investigation, now Senator Buchanan was cleared of any wrongdoing related to the Public Accounts allegations. The investigations dragged out long enough to allow the inevitable outcome to be announced without the risk of a hue and cry of a coverup for not finding him guilty of blatant political patronage leading to a breach of public trust.

CHAPTER 13

Scape Goats on Trial

D avid Nantes being charged by the Halifax police for releasing medial information and his subsequent resignation a short two weeks after Buchanan's escape to the Senate can now be put into perspective.

While Buchanan was in power, Nantes was protected by the Boss who encouraged, condoned, and supported the government's attack on my credibility through a psychiatric assessment that could only have been coordinated with Buchanan's approval. The door was now open for a new party leader to take over and Nantes would, under any other circumstances, have been a strong candidate. However now he was 'tainted tuna' and an embarrassment to the Tory establishment for spearheading an attack that backfired.

The Halifax police stalled the Nantes re-investigation until after the CBC video tapes, pursuant to the inevitable receipt of a search warrant were in their hands. The tapes were given up two hours later after Bill Donavan the station manager consulted CBC's lawyer Gavin Giles, both of whom were no doubt receiving instructions from higher up in the CBC food chain.

By handing over the tapes, Nantes' political life was finished. The police knew for more than three months what was on the tapes but waited for a couple of weeks for the smoke to clear after Buchanan's resignation to charge him.

Nantes who went on trial in January 1991 and was eventually

acquitted of the charges two months later. The court was of the opinion that the communication by Nantes that on the basis of a medical opinion recommending that I be treated out-of-province at government expense that he as Minister approved was not the kind of matter that was required to be kept secret and that he was entitled to comment and communicate on it.

They reasoned that the disclosure by the Minister divulged nothing specific relating to my medical condition but merely justified the expenditure of public funds for the purpose of providing out-of-province health services. The court believed that Nantes comments were further justified because I implied that he and the government forced me to take the out-of-province treatment when, in the court's opinion, the sole reason for the treatment was on the basis of a recommendation by a medical doctor who I had privately consulted at the urging of my family.

The government prosecutor cherry picked the information to present a case to the court that the government did not want to win. No mention was made at trial of the statements made by Nantes to the effect that the medical reports which the government relies on when it sends someone out-of-province, indicated that I left the hospital without permission.

With some digging, which would have included an interview with me about the case, the prosecutor would upon investigation of the timelines in question realize that the decision to send me away was made by my brothers John and David in consultation with Power and Donahe before I arrived at the Abbie Lane, and that the services provided in Homewood were in fact available in Nova Scotia. Dr. Teehan, the government paid doctor, was consulted by my brother John, and brought into the conspiracy, and the plan to get me out of the picture was hatched.

Although Buchanan was off the hook, his two close friends and associates, lawyer Mark Cleary and Don Power, former Deputy Minister were arraigned on 9 Oct 1991 in the wake of the RCMP Investigation.

Both men pleaded not guilty; Cleary to influence peddling related to an incident involving Millenium Masonry in June of 1990, and Power to a breach of trust by a public official for a contract he signed on Nov 22, 1989, days before his retirement.

Cleary and Power were tried separately by Nancy Bateman formally of Paterson Kitz who was appointed to the court shortly after navigating the divorce settlement with my ex-wife – covering up the Premier's involvement in the affair.

Power's lawyer was given the opportunity to object to her taking the case but did not. Possibly because both he and Power felt that Bateman would side with them. Power after all would have had indirect contact with her during the common cause of discrediting my reputation through the preparation of the filing for divorce

Power was charged with breach of trust by a public official for a contract he signed on Nov 22, 1984, to oversee hospital construction negotiated with Buchanan days before Power's retirement.

The Power contract was cancelled in the fall of 1990 after Buchanan went to the Senate. As pointed out earlier, both Donahoe and Nantes wanted to get rid of Power who had more sway with the Premier than either of them did. In June 1989 Donahue publicly stated in response to opposition questions about the Power contract that it would be ending soon.

Donahoe obviously had overlooked the fact that Power was Buchanan's man and that the contract would not end unless either Power or Buchanan wanted it to end and not before. Fifteen months later in September 1990 following Buchanan's departure to the Senate, Donahoe as Minister of Government Services was finally able to cancel the contract with Power.

Power's case was adjudicated based on opposing views on 'public trust". The defense position was that an official cannot breach a public trust by doing what he is told to do, if he is responding to orders from the person who placed him in the position of trust in the first place. The prosecution took the larger view that a public trust implies a special bond between officials and the public, and not every person in authority, such as a Premier, can give permission to break that trust.

Power testified that he went to Buchanan to tender his resignation on Sept 10, 1984, that would have taken effect two weeks later, on Sept 26th. He said Buchanan was reluctant to accept and asked him to oversee the construction of the Veteran's Memorial Hospital project.

He went on to say that the Premier asked him to draft a contract which he willingly did on terms beneficial to himself while he was still the Deputy Minister. What didn't come out at trial was that Power using his influence as a member of the Hospital Construction Management Committee held up the hospital project for six months from May when the preliminary design was submitted for approval to December when he had his contract in place to oversee the construction of the project.

Judge Bateman found Power guilty. In her ruling she stated that he used his public office for the furtherance of personal ends and that by wearing both hats, by contracting with himself and breached the trust he owed the people of Nova Scotia.

She pointed out that Power tried to serve two masters and was divided between personal and public interest, saying it was Power's duty as Deputy to determine if the department could oversee the project as had been the practice until then on all other major hospital projects or decide if for the first time an outside project manager was needed.

Bateman concluded that the duty of public officials is to the public. Proper conduct by those in public service, whether elected or otherwise, is essential to the public's confidence. The appearance of integrity is as important as integrity in fact.

In sentencing Bateman taking a swipe at Buchanan said the province is not the private enterprise of the Premier and his subordinates and fined Power $5,000.

Power and his lawyer who were looking for an absolute discharge were taken aback. Judge Bateman did not follow the script and they were forced to appeal the ruling. The Court of Appeal allowed the appeal and quashed the conviction, stating that the entire transaction, from the request for the accused to continue serving the province beyond his retirement to the completion of the contract under the stamp of approval of the Management Board, was within the law and in the public interest, and that there was no element of the transaction that could reasonably be construed as a breach of trust on the part of the accused.

The ruling is contradicted by the evidence of both Power and Buchanan whereby Buchanan asked Power to stay, not the other way around, and moreover although Power may have done a good job and conducted himself in the public interest, he was motivated primarily by his interests in the first place. The court has set a precedence open to all senior bureaucrats to follow. In what began as a breach of trust may now become the accepted and lawful practice in Nova Scotia. The good old boys look after each other.

In Cleary's case which was tried in August '92 before Bateman, he was charged with influence peddling for offering to use his friendship with Buchanan to help a newly created stone restoration masonry company win government contracts.

The trial transcript disclosed that former apprentices of Canstone who formed Millennium Masonry Ltd. after becoming fully fledged stonemasons, met with Cleary at his instigation on June 7th, a week before the Public Accounts accusations surfaced. At the meeting Clearly claimed to be a personal friend and confidant of Buchanan and related a couple of anecdotes using my name to support this connection.

Cleary recounted a story about being in Florida with certain government people and friends of Buchanan and having an opportunity to win a bet with another individual as to who would be the next Deputy Minister of Government Services. He did not, according to his story, accept the bet although he had accurate inside information as to who would be appointed. He said he later confided in the Premier of his turning down the bet. The Premier told him he should have taken it.

He then went on to tell the four stonemasons that I was having problems and was under the influence of a cult. This 'cult' business surfaces again and by stating this story to strangers when trying to impress them with his connection to the Premier he is confirming the depth and breadth of the smear campaign launched by the government with the Premier's support well before my appearance at Public Accounts.

Clearly offered to act on Millennium's behalf in exchange for equity in the company and a 20% share of the profits. Millenium countered a few days later with an offer of a finder's fee or to sell Cleary the 20% share for $20,000 which Cleary was not prepared to accept.

When Millennium told Cleary that they had been in touch with certain government ministers about work opportunities, Cleary told them that you have to go the top man (Buchanan) if you want to get anything done. His words were to the effect that they would have a better chance of obtaining government contracts with him as part of the company.

To win a conviction, the Crown had to prove that Cleary had or pretended to have influence with the government or a Minister and that there was a demand or offered to accept a benefit as consideration for cooperation, assistance, or exercise of influence in connection with the transaction of government business.

Bateman was satisfied that the Crown had proved, beyond a reasonable doubt, the essential element of the offence and found Cleary guilty as charged and fined him $4,000.

CHAPTER 14

Trying to Change the System from Within

With Buchanan's departure to the Senate, I gave serious consideration to running for office to help build back the party and clean up the pervasive patronage. I felt it was incumbent on me to help restore good government and that I had an obligation to help rebuild what was torn apart by my exposure of the inside workings of the political system.

Sometimes you have to demolish something before you can build back something new. My goal was to rid the province of corruption by first shining a light on the inner workings of government and refocusing efforts in a more transparent and populist way through communication and cooperation to serve the public interest.

The bid for leadership would have to rely on the disenfranchised grass roots Tories who'd welcome a new leader from outside the establishment, because there would be few if any allies from within the ranks of the conservative caucus.

Once these aspirations were made public the Tories circled the wagons and made it next to impossible to get a party membership let alone put my name in the hat as a candidate in the leadership convention. The straw that broke the camel's back was the new rule that the deposit required to run as a candidate for leadership was increased to $10,000, an insurmountable amount to raise under the circumstances.

Behind the scenes the party brass had to ensure that any platform that would give me an opportunity to expose the blatant government patronage that was the stock and trade of their existence had to be blocked, the Conservative Party had had enough of me.

Party membership was open to all resident supporters of the Progressive Conservative Party acceptable to the executive. The key words here being 'acceptable to the executive' a hurdle that I was not going to overcome no matter how much grassroot support was out there.

The initial reaction to my expression of interest from a few high-profile provincial ministers ranged from incredulity to icy rejection. Government Services Minister Terry Donahoe dismissed the idea that I could even make a credible candidate. My former boss George Moody was more blunt saying that I would not be the kind of individual that he could support, which in my view says a lot about Moody, while others simply said no comment.

Donahoe pontificated that cabinet ministers who were vying for the top job had to decide whether they were carrying too much baggage from Buchanan's scandal plagued government before entering the race to replace him. Donahoe, a top contender accepted his own advice and chose not to run for the 'sake of the party' – or was it to protect his deep dark secrets.

The three contenders in the race from the Buchanan cabinet were Industry Minister Donald Cameron, Minister of Tourism Rollie Thornhill, and Attorney General Tom McInnis.

Cameron was a black and white kind of guy who campaigned on the promise of being a new and different political broom to change customs and political practices in Nova Scotia while apposing patronage.

Buchanan and Cameron were not close especially because of Cameron's tendency to take a hard line on issues without showing deference to his boss or his party. I recall during the Public Accounts session when the initial corruption accusations were made seeing Cameron from the corner of my eye standing in the doorway taking in every word of my testimony as if he was plotting something.

Thornhill was a longtime colleague, and close political ally of Buchanan. Thornhill, the most capable and experienced of the lot was perhaps one of the people Donahoe was referring to in his unsolicited pontification because of an ongoing RCMP investigation for a deal Thornhill made with four banks to write off personal debts.

Tom McInnis had earned a high-profile reputation as Attorney General for his role in cleaning up the tattered Nova Scotia justice system. However, his preferred attire of cowboy boots and hats gave him the moniker "Cowboy Tom" that did not resonate with the east coast mentality no matter how competent and capable he may have been.

Although Cameron had the support of most caucus and cabinet ministers, no candidate had an overwhelming lead however Cameron maintained a slim majority throughout the convention eventually carried the day defeating his opponents to become the party leader and premier. Cameran had a little over two years to complete Buchanan's term before he had to call a provincial election in May 1993.

Meanwhile Vince MacLean, the holier than thou, combative, political street brawler's admission to taking $60,000 a year in extra salary and benefits from a secretly administered Liberal trust fund had to resign in 1992 as Liberal Party leader.

This paved the way for Mayor John Savage to succeed him and take over as the Liberal leader. Savage was a popular and well-respected Mayor of Dartmouth with a strong support base built up by serving the community as a family doctor.

In my political naivety I continued to look for opportunities of serving the public and during the campaign met privately with Thornhill at his home in Dartmouth and then with Cameron in Pictou County to test if there was any role for me in government. Both were cordial in listening to my aspirations but neither offered any hope or support.

Cameron campaigned on his record of making significant reforms since assuming office in 1991, however this was not enough to shake off the allegations of patronage from the Buchanan regime that he was a part of.

The Liberals under their new leader John Savage won a landslide victory gaining 19 seats promising to end pork-barrel politics and introduce a new style of governing focusing on job creation.

Shortly after Savage's election win as party leader and before he had won a seat in the legislature, I met with him in his Dartmouth office offering my services as one who knew the inner workings of government to continue the shared vision of establishing more openness and transparency.

Unlike the caring, considerate facade shown to the public to win the election, Savage, as his name implied, showed me the side of his personality that came across as aloof, arrogant, and condescending. He wanted nothing to do with the idea and left no hope for a role in his government.

Somewhat disillusioned I shared my experience with a former colleague who was not surprised by the reception from Savage saying that not only did I turn the modus operandi of the Conservative party on its head leading to its fall from power, I was an anathema to all political parties as they all operate the same way.

He went on to say that no one since Joseph Howe, a journalist and arguably one of Nova Scotia's greatest politicians who had exposed corruption and put in place sweeping government reforms has done as much to change the way government operates until I came forward.

The first year of the final decade of the 20th century is destined to be remembered as a year of change in Nova Scotia. It was a year of power lost and a year of public awakening and a year of long-kept secrets finally told, leading in part to a more open and honest government.

CHAPTER 15

In the Public Eye

O f several interviews to various newspapers the following is representative of my thoughts and aspirations during the heat of the battle was published by the Halifax Mail Star in July 1990.

Zareski's Mission

Michael Zareski has been in the spotlight in Nova Scotia since mid-June, when he made startling allegations of widespread patronage and corruption within the Buchanan government. The former government services deputy minister talked earlier this week about how he got into the civil service, when he first saw patronage at work, his political aspirations, and spiritual ponderings which have led him to a belief in reincarnation, and to experiments with past-life regressions where he has seen himself as philosopher Thomas Aquinas. Here is the text of the interview with Features Writer Rob Mills.

Rob Mills: How are you holding up after several weeks in the public eye?

Michael Zareski:" I'm feeling great...no stress or strain. I don't feel any difficulty at all with what I'm doing is right, and when you're doing the right thing, your conscious is clear, and you have no stress to burden you."

R.M.: To start at the beginning, how did you become a civil servant?

Zareski: "Going back to university, I had been working on summer jobs with the Department of Transportation as a surveyor, and in 1972 when I graduated, I had anticipated getting a job as an engineer in the Department of Transportation, but I wasn't successful and that fall I had an opportunity of going to work with the Department of Public Works. I was interviewed, as a matter of fact, by Don Power, the deputy minister, and started in September 1972."

R.M.: There are rumors that patronage played a part in your hiring because your sister's brother-in-law was then highway minister Garnet Brown.

Zareski: "If patronage did play a role in that appointment, he didn't get me on as an engineer in his department - a number of my family - brothers and sisters' 'knew Mr. Power, and I think through conversations they indicated to him that I was a graduate engineer - whether or not Garnet Brown pulled strings behind the scenes, I have no idea."

R.M.: When did you first see patronage at work?

Zareski: "It's hard to say. When you're early on in your career you're isolated from this sort of thing. You do your job and if you are working on a project or a building all the major decisions are made at the top and you just carry on with your work - you don't necessarily know how appointments are made - I think to a great extent even the staff today in the Department of Government Services have been isolated from knowledge of how it works at the top. I suppose when I became deputy minister, I saw how it truly worked.

"I knew that certainly there were different players in the game from the 70's to the 80's - certain architects that we worked with when the Liberals were in power, we didn't work with when the Conservatives were in power and certain businessmen in all fields - we didn't work with when government changed."

R.M.: What was the first incident that seriously bothered you?

Zareski: "I think it started off the day I was appointed deputy minister when I was called to the Premier's Office and I had a meeting with the Premier and he indicated to me words to the effect that I am in a very sensitive department and sometimes I may be asked to do things I may not be comfortable with, but would I go along with it because that's politics and that's how politics works. I knew there and then that the style had been set and not knowing how pervasive that may become, I thought I could certainly go along with it providing that it didn't' violate my ethics in dealing with things."

R.M.: When did it first violate those ethics?

Zareski: "I always said what I thought was right and in cases where we had a serious disagreement I would make sure that they (ministers) insisted that I do something ; but there were cases where I was saying to myself 'Even if they tell me to do this, I'm not going to do this and I'll resign if necessary' and I think the biggest issue was the thing with Mark Cleary and the Canstone affair. I think at that point in time I was prepared to hand in my resignation if I was forced in some way to keep him involved with Canstone."

R.M.: Would he have left Canstone if you hadn't taken a stand?

Zareski: "Truly, I don't think so. I think it was my pressure that caused that to happen."

R.M.: Did you ever consider giving a reporter an anonymous tip about patronage deals?

Zareski: "I don't work that way - I feel that if people have something to say, they should stand up and identify themselves."

R.M.: When did you first plan to make your allegations before the public accounts committee?

Zareski: "When I was invited to attend public accounts, and that was about two or three weeks beforehand. All along I had been preparing myself to take the government to court, and what I was looking for was the motive the government had for doing what they did in sending me off to the Homewood institution for psychiatric evaluation. They were saying that it was because of the concern of my family, yet I knew there was more to it because they were saying they had nothing to do with it and I was getting information that they had a lot to do with it, so I was trying to establish why they want to do this. Most people, if I'm separating from my wife or you're separating from your wife, your employer doesn't get involved in it, and I couldn't understand why the government was getting involved in this private matrimonial affair. In trying to establish motive, I said 'Well that's it, I was a thorn in their side. Every time they wanted something done, I was saying 'No, that's not ethical or that's not right - if we have a tendering policy, we should abide by it' - and they didn't seem to like that. They have two sets of rules - one for their friends and one for everybody else and I didn't see it that way."

R.M.: If there weren't problems with your personal life, and you were still deputy minister, would your testimony have been different?

Zareski: "I had told the government I was planning to leave just before this time in any case, because I just couldn't see myself continuing on under that kind of system - whether or not they would have even invited me to public accounts. I don't know, and perhaps I wouldn't have gone into the detail because I would not have had reason to think it all out to put it into context. I would have been busy off on another career."

R.M.: What was your motive in giving such testimony?

Zareski: "I think the greatest motive is to see justice done, and although attention is being put on Michael Zareski at this point in time, what they did to me they could have done to anybody, because it was so slick the way they tried to discredit me. I think it showed me that anybody who bucks the system is going to receive retaliation from these people, and that's why I see a lot of yes men in government. They're afraid to stand up and say what's right, and I don't think that people should have that kind of fear in any of their operations - my motive is to see a more open government, because I see how pervasive they can be with stifling openness."

R.M.: Was there an element of revenge that you wanted to get back at the government?

Zareski: "I think an element of - again I'm going to say seek justice, not necessarily revenge. Revenge is something taken out of control, and you say things or do things that have no basis in fact, in some cases. I'm only seeking justice."

R.M.: Did you seek advice from anyone before testifying?

Zareski: "I didn't seek anybody's advice - I guess the biggest counsel I had was my own conscience."

R.M.: Were you at all worried that the testimony would cut you off completely from a system you had been part of for years?

Zareski: "I was cut off from my future in that system, and even from businessmen who worked outside of the government per se, on the day that they sent me into the Homewood Centre, because the way I was treated by my friends and my associates was completely different from that day, and I saw a detailed and thorough system of trying to discredit me all through that summer. Even when I got out with the proof that there was nothing wrong with me, that wasn't acceptable to them. They still persisted with the rumours of a nervous breakdown and that he can't be trusted or whatever. They continued to support my wife without conversation or discussion with me, they wouldn't answer my letters, or return phone calls to my lawyer, or anything all through that time - they can take away everything from me, but they can't take away my integrity. When that's all that's left with an individual, you're going to come back and fight."

R.M.: Why is no one else speaking out?

Zareski: "For fear. If someone spoke out earlier on, and we've seen it happen where opposition parties would speak up and ask questions about activities and the government would cover it up so slick - we say what happened with Billy Joe MacLean and so on; only when he was convicted of wrongful acts, did they get rid of him. All the time that he was doing it and the government knew he was doing it, they said everything was fine until he got caught. That seems to be their criteria; we don't mind whatever our ministers or the government does, but at the point of time that they're caught and convicted, then we'll get rid of them. The ethics within government has been pretty shoddy all the way through."

R.M.: Before all this happened, how would you describe your relationship with John Buchanan?

Zareski: "I think we had a mutual respect for each other, and I think that he knew where I was coming from, and I knew where he was coming from, and I could accommodate him on finding jobs for a certain category of employee within government, but when it came to the most senior levels I felt it was necessary and important to get the very best people in there that were qualified and went through the civil service procedures and so on. I think we understood that with one another and we worked in that way, and I think he understood when I was saying no, I couldn't do it, then he knew I wasn't necessarily going along with the tune he was playing."

R.M.: Did you like one another?

Zareski: "Well, let me just leave it as a healthy respect for one another."

R.M.: Did he ever discuss with you how patronage fits in his government?

Zareski: "Only that very first day that I was appointed, and I wouldn't expect the Premier to lay it out. He's too smart of a man to say 'Look, this is a patronage decision, we want you to go along with it.' You read between the line in these situations and these affairs."

R.M.: What do you think the Premier's attitude towards patronage is?

Zareski: "I think he honestly believes it's the best way to conduct government for himself, because I believe that his first end is himself, the second end maybe the party, and I don't think the governing of the people of Nova Scotia is paramount in his mind. Look at the policies this government has put in place. I don't think you will see very many - you see what's happening with education, with the hospitals, protest after protest this year at the House of Assembly, where the people of Nova Scotia are saying we've had enough - it was unprecedented, the number of marches on the legislature, and a good government doesn't have that kind of backlash from the people."

R.M: Nova Scotia has been called the "Deep North" a comparison to corrupt southern U.S. states. Do you think we're innately corrupt due to the small population?

Zareski: "First of all, I love Nova Scotia, and I see a tremendous potential in Nova Scotia, and my sense is that the people of Nova Scotia are good, honest, hardworking people. Somebody told me that if you take the population and break them down into thirds, one third would steel, another third would not steel one way or another - they could go either way - and the last third would never do it, in no way, shape, or form. They say what is happening here is that the third in the middle is following the lead of whoever is in power, and it seems to be that if you are led by someone or a group of people who feels there is nothing wrong with patronage and this kind of system, or that you serve yourself before the people, well then that's the kind of government you're going to have. If you have someone there for honest open government, the third in the middle are going to follow that as well. We've been innovators in a lot of things; we've been innovators in government in Canada and I think we can be innovators in this change to an open government as well - I have a belief in the innate goodness of people."

R.M.: You've talked about running for office. Are you serious?

Zareski: "I believe my future will lead me to a political life, yes."

R.M.: Do you think you could fit into party structures which sometimes demand loyalty over personal integrity?

Zareski: "My philosophy is that you don't vote for the party, you vote for the man, and you vote for the man whose integrity matches the integrity that you as a voter want to see - If we vote for the man with ideas of change and fresh thoughts, then he can mould and change the party so I think that politicians of the future will be those who represent the aspirations and desires of the individual, and I think ethics is going to be the biggest issue in the future of politics."

R.M.: Would you run through an established party?

Zareski: "It could be through an established party, but I think the candidates of the future will be candidates who will express their freedom of thought. I don't think it's right, for instance, to have a vote on a very important issue and have to follow party lines. If there were any votes in any party I would be involved with, I would adamantly insist that each individual be given the right to represent his people and himself through his freedom of consciousness."

R.M.: What would you say to somebody who would call you an unrealistic idealist?

Zareski: "I don't think it's unrealistic to strive for truth and goodness in the world. Something's got to turn around, doesn't it? We need people who say, 'Well here's the way it is, but here's the way it should be ' If that's called idealism that's fine - if that's called unrealistic, then I don't accept that. I think it is realistic to hope for betterment because innately people are good."

R.M.: Do you see yourself as eventually taking that kind of leadership role?

Zareski: "Yes."

R.M.: Would you describe yourself as in any way partisan?

Zareski: "No. I have never been a partisan. I have always been an individual, and I will, I think, gravitate towards the party that I can be most effective in."

R.M: Do you see yourself running in the next provincial election?

Zareski: 'I would say that that's a possibility because I think there are going to be a lot of things happening between now and the next provincial election that will give me those opportunities."

R.M.: What sort of things?

Zareski: "Well, I don't think the government is going to be able to survive from the exposition of the depth of patronage that goes on, and I think that people are going to stand up and take notice that things have to change, and they're going to be looking for people who are willing to stand up and change things, and I can see that that's going to happen; and I think that not only myself but many others are going to come forward and say we want our government or our politicians or our elected representatives to represent us in this way - that the people have to be heard."

R.M.: Would you like to be premier of this province some day?

Zareski: "Well, my whole style in life has been to go towards goals and aspirations. I remember when I first started off in Public Works back in '72, I indicated to my wife at that time that I'm going to be the deputy minister of the department, and I became the deputy minister; so anything that I've put my mind to I've been able to achieve, and if I get into politics my goal or aspiration will be to be premier of the province to serve the people through that role, and I can certainly say that that is something that I can see for me and that I will work towards."

R.M.: What concrete changes would you make to eat at the roots of patronage?

Zareski: "I think the first thing is that the debates in the legislature must be open to the media and to the public through the media, and I think that will let people know what is happening."

R.M.: You mean having cameras in the house?

Zareski: "That's right. You know they talked for three years about ethics within government, and we're going to put an ethics package out for the MLAs. Nothing has happened with that, and I think that that should be done; and people have to be listened to more - also, amalgamate some departments that are competing with each other. We're only a small province of less than a million people, yet we have something like 22 departments and 22 ministers, and I think we could do a lot better with a lot less."

R.M.: There has been a lot of talk about your belief in Rosicrucianism. Can you give me a brief description of it?

Zareski: "The Rosicrucian order is a world-wide fraternity of men and women who study mysticism, science, and the arts, and try to understand God's natural laws and His spiritual laws and how man fit and lives within the influences of these laws - many of the greatest men and women were Rosicrucians - I'm thinking of people like Benjamin Franklin, Debussy, the composer, Socrates, and Plato back in ancient history were Rosicrucians. People who philosophize about the meanings and mysteries of life, and who have a belief that there's more to life than what you perceive through your five senses, lead themselves on to these concepts that are established by the Rosicrucian order. What the Rosicrucians want you to do is to come to your own individual belief, not on any dogma or any information they say you must or must not believe, but to investigate and come to your own truth."

R.M.: How were you introduced to the order?

Zareski: "I've always been somewhat philosophical, and I would have philosophical conversations with friends and acquaintances from time to time ... we (a friend and Zareski) were at a Christmas party philosophizing about the meaning of life, and he said you might be interested in this (Rosicrucian) book - and I joined the order to find out more about it.

R.M.: How long ago was this?

Zareski: "I think about four years ago."

R.M.: Is belief in reincarnation an integral part of Rosicrucianism?

Zareski: "Not an integral part. There are many Rosicrucians who believe in it, and many who don't believe in it. It's up to how you feel about it yourself - I think if they do say anything, it's that you must keep an open mind about the possibility of anything."

R.M.: Your own contemplation has led you to a belief in reincarnation?

Zareski: "That's correct."

R.M.: How?

Zareski: "I've read a lot on reincarnation, and I've had some past life regressions done that would bring past lives to my attention, and I can see how our personalities evolve through many lives. And also, I read the Bible and I can interpret the veiled messages of reincarnation within the Bible. When Jesus would say, 'Who is it that they say I am,' and the answer is some say you're Elijah, some say Jeremiah, some say one of the prophets, and he said to Peter 'Well who is it that you think I am ?' and Peter says, 'I say you are the Christ, the son of the living God.' So, Jesus was saying to them 'It's important who I am in this life, not who I may have been in the last life or past lives.' Jesus keeps saying we must be born again, and if you take that literally, the soul never dies - the soul comes from God and goes back to God through experiencing many lives to come to perfection."

R.M.: Do you think past lives influence what you are doing now?

Zareski: "Past lives have influence on what's happening with everybody who is here today, whether or not they believe it, that's up to themselves. It has an influence on who you are in the present; you see people who, at two or three years old, are child prodigies and play piano or are musical or whatever. Where did that ability come from? It's not genetic, in a lot of cases, because the family has had nothing to do with these sorts of things. And when you're in touch with yourself, you're closer to the character and personality that has built up over many lifetimes."

R.M.: Through past live experiences, and gaining insight into what some of those past lives may be, do you believe that you may have been a saint in an earlier life?

Zareski: "When I was at the Homewood Centre, one of the doctors there did a past life regression. We would talk philosophically about these things, and he said, 'Would you be interested in one?' and I said 'Sure.' One afternoon when he had no appointments, he said come on over and we'll do one. The past life that came to me was the life of a saint. I think we both found it quite interesting, and it seemed to indicate that - I was leading myself in this life to do the sort of things that will change people's outlook and views on life. Now, I didn't make that up. Here was a medical doctor who did past life regressions, and this was the life that came out in the course of the past life regression."

R.M.: Can you tell me how that session worked?

Zareski: "Well - he asked me to relax and breathe calmly and deeply and imagine myself in a very relaxed, comfortable setting, in my mind's eye, maybe it was by a lake or the ocean or whatever, and he indicated that in the cosmic, time and space have no boundaries so your consciousness can go wherever it wants in time and space. It's just a matter of imagination allowing itself to go. He's hypnotizing me while he is doing this, I believe, and putting me in a relaxed, altered state and working with my consciousness and suggesting that I go back in time and space and stop at a particular time and tell him what images are coming through my imagination; and I started to do that and I could see these pictures coming to my imagination and I was describing what I was doing and where I was and the events of that point in time. He asked, 'Who are you?' and I mentioned what my name was, and he asked, 'Well why did this particular life come to you - for what purpose were you brought back to this life for your review?' - and we discussed that, and that session took about half an hour.

R.M.: When the session is over, can you remember those events?

Zareski: "Oh yes, quite clearly."

R.M.: What time period had you gone back to?

Zareski: "I was back in the middle ages."

R.M.: And what were your physical surroundings?

Zareski: "I was in an institution like a library, and I was writing and studying and establishing philosophical concepts, I suppose."

R.M.: What name did you give yourself?

Zareski: "The name that came forward was Thomas Aquinas."

R.M.: So, in what you have come to understand, would that suggest that the spirit of Thomas Aquinas has passed through generations and surfaced in you?

Zareski: "I wouldn't necessarily say that - it's a very deep concept - we're all fragments of a divine soul - it's difficult to get into it in a short conversation, but it is not exactly as you perceive it to be."

R.M.: Nova Scotia is both politically and religiously conservative. Are you concerned that your spiritual beliefs will undermine your credibility?

Zareski: "No, not one way or the other, I am who I am, I believe what I believe, and I don't think I have to justify my beliefs. I think we are living in a free society, and we have laws that say you and I can believe whatever we wish to believe. Whether or not I believe I was Thomas Aquinas or whoever in a past life, whether or not I believe in reincarnation, should make no difference whatsoever with what I am doing in this life. I think people get mixed up and confused about those sorts of things. More than half of the world's population today believes in reincarnation - you go in any bookstore and they're full of these sorts of things. People seem to be crying for more information as to who are we, why are we, what makes us the way we are, and I think that they are trying to break away from their religion in a box - spirituality guided by the church. They want to come to verify their own truths for themselves through their own experiences."

R.M.: Knowing for instance, that in the Annapolis Valley there is a strong Baptist Church, and Roman Catholicism in Cape Breton and the Antigonish area, and that these churches have a specific dogma, I'm wondering if you are confident people evaluating you as a politician will be able to step outside their religious dogmas?

Zareski: "Well, that is going to be their particular problem because I as well am a very devout Christian and a follower of Catholicism, but I don't necessarily accept dogma. I think that dogma is saying, 'You cannot think for yourself, you must think what we tell you to think.' and I don't think people now accept that. They want to live their own life, make their own choices, and grow and learn from the successes and failures they make for themselves."

R.M.: What's been the toughest thing for you in the past few years?

Zareski: "This whole business around the Homewood Centre, realizing that I couldn't go back to my wife and family or back to the government, and to accept that the government had perpetrated this whole thing. That was difficult, but once I accepted that this is what happened, then everything became positive again and I knew I had to seek justice."

CHAPTER 16

Persona Non Grata

After my ties with the government were severed, it was clear that it would be necessary to start a new life and get a job. For several months, contacts were made with several individuals and companies in and around Sydney and Halifax with whom I had developed good working relationships over the years.

Regrettably phone calls were not returned or were abruptly cut off. The government campaign to blackball me well before my appearance at Public Accounts had taken effect. The rumor mill and subsequent media attention would have been too much for any employer to deal with. Nonetheless my attempts to find work continued, applying for advertised positions for engineering and management roles that were commensurate with my skills and experience.

By the end of the year my rejection file was inches thick, however there were a couple of promising job opportunities that almost resulted in employment. One involved a senior position with an aerospace organization and when interviewed on the phone it was suggested that I would be perfect for the job and was asked if we could meet in Halifax for a follow-up face-to-face discussion.

A few days later at a popular watering hole on Spring Garden Road in Halifax. I arrived at the designated time and waited for more than a half hour before resigning myself to the fact that my contact was a no-show.

I was about to leave with barely enough money for gas to drive back to Cape Breton, when the man in the next table, who recognized me from the media, introduced himself and praised me for the courage for standing up to the government. He then pulled out his cheque book and wrote out a $500 gift which goes a long way when you're broke.

My follow up calls to the aerospace contact who set up the interview with the hope of rescheduling were not returned.

The next opportunity came from a call with an up-and-coming land developer who I had worked closely with over the years while I was with the government. He was an aggressive go getter who was following the ongoing saga in the news and said he was not in the least concerned about hiring me and that he would have his office call in a day or so to set up a start date for work. After a few days of waiting for the call from his office, my calls to confirm our arrangement were not answered or returned.

In both cases, interventions were made to block these opportunities. I assumed the intervention with the aerospace organization was from someone within the government; with the land developer, I subsequently found out from a reliable source that it was my brother David who made the call to my developer friend and put the kibosh to the opportunity.

After dozens of rejections, I finally got the message that people like me who expose wrongdoing about activities within an organization become untouchables. To employers, whistleblowers are troublemakers to hush, punish or banish to some career gulag.

When faced with the loss of livelihood for ethically doing the right thing as opposed to keeping silent and going along with the way the government operated, it boiled down to pitting ethics against the practicality of silence and for me silence was not practical it was emotional lobotomy.

Had I stayed in government, the apathy experienced towards my work would have diminished my initiative, and ability to succeed. This decreased depth of intensity towards life would have turned me into a zombie and I'm convenience I would not be alive today had I not spoken out.

The workforce is full of obedient soldiers who are taught from childhood to take direction from external authorities - to go along to get along - this was not me. Biting the hand that feeds you takes a special kind of courage. However, in my idealistic outlook on life, the hand that feeds me is not in the material realm, it is in the spiritual realm it is the hand of God as experienced through my guides, guardian angels and Higher Self.

Although the intensity of the constant media attention with requests for interviews from newspaper and television reporters, which had consumed my time, had subsided my attempts to get on with life as I knew it was not in the cards. I was time to live in the moment and accept what is in front of me.

CHAPTER 17

Malevolent Motives

Throughout this time, it was important to me to renew contact with my boys and although there were periodic phone calls, they were sporadic at best and all endeavors to reconnect were futile. My lawyer continued his efforts to coordinate a visit as contemplated by the divorce settlement agreement and was not able to make headway. Afterall Patricia was the gate keeper and without her approval, it didn't matter how many interventions were made, by whom, or for that matter what the boys wanted, a visit would not happen without her blessing.

This position was confirmed by a letter sent to my lawyer from Patricia's lawyer which stated that according to Mrs. Zareski the boys remain adamant that they did not wish to see their father and accused me of being the barrier to access. Upon receiving that information, I reached out to my lawyer expressing regret about the inability to deal reasonably with Mrs. Zareski and sadness over what has occurred with the relationship with my sons.

The next strategy initiated by my lawyer was to go back to court to establish access through a court appointed mediation service at no cost to either party. He encouraged me not to give up even though up until now attempts have been blocked at every turn. Patricia's lawyer eventually wrote back to my lawyer stating that Mrs. Zareski will not agree to mediation services and recommended that I continue to attempt communication.

This in my view was simply another stalling tactic which would get me nowhere.

My lawyer moved forward to prepare documents to file in court to obtain more liberal access to the boys. To support his preparation, I sent him a summary of the attempts made over the last eighteen months to make contact with my sons and provide him with an understanding of the circumstances and events which had occurred.

I could not understand how the very strong and loving father-son relationship that I had with my boys could have deteriorated to such an extent that they were fearful of me and did not wish to have anything further to do with me. It was obvious that it was not from something I had done in their presence because the last time I was with them in the Abbie Lane Hospital we got along very well.

It is my conclusion that their fear of me was established during my absence from them while they were in the care and custody of their mother. I belief that their mother purposely and calculatedly had turned the boys against me. This was confirmed by statements made to me by my sister Mary who told me that Patricia had no compunction about suggesting to anyone present and that would care to listen to her that I was mentally unstable and that I had tried to kill her.

This was done in the presence of the boys and conformed to the contents of her early divorce petition affidavits on those allegations even though in her discovery testimony she admitted that the allegation was baseless and accepted that the discharge papers from Homewood showed no indication of mental illness.

The open hostility, as evidenced by my contacts with my brothers John and David, towards me was further assurance I would never see my boys through them because I was informed that they did not feel that I deserved to see the boys again. And Dr. Teehan's report since it was issued was continually used to prevent access on the basis that the boys must decide. However, before the report I could not see them until Dr. Teehan's assessment was done.

The report suited her circumstances, and she used it continually to her advantage. Even when the boys did express an interest in seeing me, they mysteriously changed their minds and, in most cases, this change of mind was communicated through their mother. Through the direct and indirect intervention their minds were changed for them. I also suspect that many of the communications sent by Patricia's lawyer regarding the boy were again answered by their mother with no input from the boys.

Although it was difficult, it was necessary to accept that the boys were mature enough to decide what was best while living at home under their mother's care and supervision. In order to maintain the status quo, they decided not to rock the boat for now, and went along with their mothers wishes. Mrs. Zareski did not want my involvement with the boys and did whatever she could to prevent that from happening.

She would not agree to an earlier assessment by refusing to cost share it. She removed the boys from the home in mid-July on my trip to visit them so that the visit could not take place. She called my brother and neighbor to the home at the time of another visit to prevent me from seeing them. She intercepted telephone calls that I had prearranged with the boys to indicate that they did not want to talk to me.

In the alternative she could have encouraged the re-establishment of our relationship but had not done so because it would be inconsistent with the stand already taken against me. Finally, she had refused to go along with the latest attempt at mediation and took the stance that she knew what was best and would decide. for them.

Finally in mid-March my hopes were rekindled in getting back on track to resolve the impasse; an order was received following the successful application made by Doug Stevenson for the court appointed mediation services.

A counselor from The Family Services Association of Nova Scotia was designated to provide mediation services to address the issue of access between me and my two boys. A series of individual and joint interviews were conducted between late April and May 1991.

There were reports coming back to me at the time that the mediation sessions were underway that Patricia expressed her concern for the boys to my family, wishing that they would resume their relationship with me sometime in the future.

She also appeared to be open to a previous condition of the divorce settlement that initially provided for supervised access by way of one of my siblings in attendance. Patricia's expressions of concern were not consistent with her actions, which over the last two years spoke louder than her words.

At the end of the mediation sessions the counsellor conveyed the wishes of the boys who did not support making contact with me. I was right back where I started on the access front with little or no hope for change in the foreseeable future.

Fortunately, back-channel communications were kept open with my mother and supportive siblings who kept me informed as to the welfare and activities of the boys who were able to spend a lot of time with them and were included in all of the joint family activities with their cousins - my nieces, and nephews. This feedback included information from their schools which indicated that both boys were doing extremely well and were an asset to their classes.

All the while that the mediation services were underway Patricia was expressing through her lawyer that she was not satisfied with the terms of the divorce settlement which ordered that upon the sale of the matrimonial home the proceeds would be split 50/50 with me. Her lawyer wrote to my lawyer stating that she would be making application to reverse this ruling and throw everything into issue.

Patricia on the one hand would agree that the house had to be sold and on the other delayed putting it on the market. The delay in selling caused her to fall behind with mortgage payments and to resolve that matter would request through the courts that funds from my pension plan be released to bring those payments out of arrears. Slowly but surely these funds were being depleted and would eventually disappear.

On top of that, Revenue Canada was on my case charging me for income tax arrears from the 1988 tax year. In my subsequent income tax submission, I claimed the amount of my salary which was paid to Patricia at the time of our separation under the alimony or separation allowance provision of the Income Tax Act and this settled the previous year's arrears and provided a tax return of a few thousand dollars.

Months later in January 1991 while in the middle of attempt to gain access to the children and support Patricia with payment of mortgage arrears Revenue Canada informed me of their intent to review the 1989 Income tax claim regarding Alimony and Maintenance. They subsequently disallowed the claim and sent a Notice of Reassessment in an amount of just under $10,000 for that year and to top that off a Notice of Assessment for the 1990 tax year which included the fifty thousand in pension monies, the bulk of which was transferred to support Patricia with the balance frozen by the court and the monies held in trust.

Requests for reconsideration outlining the particular circumstances of my case were made to Mulrooney's Minister of Finance Otto Jelinek and his deputy minister Pierre Gravelle fell on deaf ears.

There was no doubt in my mind that they were aware of the political allegations that resulted in Mulrooney providing a safe haven for his friend Buchanan in the Senate and would not have taken an unbiased or objective view to my case under those circumstances. The only practical alternative left open for me was to declare bankruptcy.

In April 1990, two months prior to the Public Accounts hearing, Glen Hanam along with Brendon Yazer and others formed the 'Michael Zareski Support Society' through which some donations, but mostly moral support was provided to assist me through my ordeals with the government.

Jack Yazer, Brendon's father was a prominent Sydney businessman, and a founding member and chair of the Cape Breton Regional Hospital Foundation, so I thought it odd at the time, especially with the public controversy my earlier statements caused about the hospital delay, that Brendon would support and befriend me.

Brendon and I were working together on a community development proposal for the Johnstown Community Centre in Richmond County located about an hour south of where we lived in Sydney. In our travels we got along pretty well, and he was a sympathetic ear with whom I shared the circumstances around my departure from government, my stay at Homewood, and the divorce from my wife. When Alexandra and I decided to get married after her divorce from her husband was finalized, I asked Brendan to be my best man which he happily agreed to do.

Since our time together I noticed that Alexandra experienced bouts of lethargy and dizziness which eventually led to a diagnosed of multiple sclerosis after her optometrist detected a lesion on the optic nerve during a routine eye examination. Knowing that when divorced from her husband she would need support and companionship and given our shared interest, I was more than willing to be there for her as she had been for me.

The wedding was a well-attended event held at the St. Anne United church in the community of North River Bridge where Alexandra was born; and to my pleasant surprise it was attended by a number of siblings who did not buy into the narrative being broadcast about my state of mind.

On the drive to the church while crossing the Seal Island Bridge in Bras D'Or, Brendan told me that he carried a handgun in his vehicle and that he was hired to kill me but couldn't follow through with it after getting to know me. With what I had been through up to now, I was not a bit surprised by this confession and not wanting to provoke the situation, simply brushed it off with a comment to the effect of 'Let's put that behind us, we have a wedding to attend to'. As the saying goes, 'Protect me from my friends, my enemies I can look after myself.' After the wedding, Brendon and I parted ways.

Alexandra and I left Sydney and moved to Indian Brook in Victoria County, Cape Breton to look after her aging widowed aunt who needed full time home care assistance. Her aunt's property adjacent to MacDonald's Pond was located on a secluded stretch of the 185-mile-long Cabot Trail. In years past her aunt offered tourist cabin accommodations to visitors of this scenic highway that loops around the Cape Breton Highlands National Park on the northern tip of the island. The move provided a welcome relief from the constant onslaught of media looking for the latest scoop. With events settling down, this allowed more time to establish contact with my boys, and for finding something to do with my life which had been put on hold for the time being.

One of the projects taken on was the demolition of the tourist cabins which had fallen into a state of disrepair over the years. One morning while removing the roof shingles I noticed a car parked on the shoulder of the road some 500 yards or so down the highway by the shore of the pond. I got off the roof and walked towards the car to investigate. As I got closer it was apparent that the driver was in that car and when he saw me approaching, he backed up, turned around, and with tires squealing took off. The getaway happened so quickly that I could not get a license plate number to identify the vehicle.

At lunchtime I went back into the house and related the story and was told that the car had been there for a couple of days. So, the surveillance which was suspected in Sydney had moved to Indian Brook, but because of the remote location, the stakeout was much harder to conceal. My suspicions were that the government was behind this and that it was not over with them. I became more concerned that they may try something to finish what they started and get even with me.

My concerns were reinforced a few days later when a friend from Sydney called, quite upset with concerns for my safety, and related a vivid dream from the night before that woke her from sleep. In her dream, she described the Indian Brook house that I was living in with a large neon sign mounted on the roof, flashing the words DANGER, DANGER, DANGER in bright red letters. Although my friend had not seen the property, she described it very accurately.

Prompted by the message, steps were taken to protect myself. I applied for a license to own a firearm and acquired a shotgun and kept it loaded by my bed at night. The license was applied for as a message to those who were surveilling me to know that I was armed.

In another incident a few weeks later, I was woken by my dog who went ballistic in the middle of the night barking frantically. She sensed something or somebody outside in the yard and upon investigation nothing was detected.

After the earlier incidents of the stake out vehicle speeding away and my friend's dream, I decided to take further precautions. At times when I would have to drive go for groceries, appointments or whatever rather than follow the direct route, an alternate way would be taken, and on one occasion when prompted by my gut feelings I drove all the way around the Cabot Trail, hours out of my way, just to avoid being intercepted. Could it be that Brendon was back to finish the job?

CHAPTER 18

Peace and Tranquility

I was somewhat familiar with this part of Cape Breton having been involved with the expansion of the Gaelic College in St. Ann's some twenty years earlier to the improvements made to the Cape Smoke Ski hill to host the alpine events for the 1987 Canada Winter Games and managing the annual winter works program for the provincially owned Keltic Lodge in Ingonish for a number of years.

My presence in the community was generally welcomed among both prominent groups; the "Locals" as represented by Alexandra a descendants from a steady in migration of Gaelic speaking Scots mostly from the islands of Lewis and Harris creating homesteads and small farms on the shores and in the hills around St. Ann's in the early 1800s, and the "Come-from-Aways", who in the early 1970's settled the "down north" communities that stretched along the Cabot Trail and its side roads from the South Haven turnoff to the foot of Cape Smokey, a distance of 72 kilometers.

It may sound counter intuitive, but many Cape Bretoners refer to communities along the northeast coast of Victoria County, as "down north", a fall back from the days of the coastal sailing vessels tacking into the winds coming down from the north.

The area is known for its beauty, with steep hills stretching into the Cape Breton Highlands and several rivers emptying into St. Ann's Bay and the Atlantic. Renowned for trout and salmon fishing the area has a thriving lobster fishery, some lumbering and several small businesses, studio craft and gift shops from Goose Cove to Wreck Cove testify to the creative initiatives of those who have come to this area determined to stay.

The area offered me peace, tranquility, and a simple way of life, living hand to mouth day-to-day, always with a roof over my head and three meals a day and the opportunity to help out in the community wherever and whenever I could.

One of the most rewarding volunteer activities was working with a group of locals and come-from-aways to support and encourage the incorporation of the St Ann's Bay Development Association in 1992.

One of the first goals of the association was to document existing community assets and to engage the community in discussion about natural resource management, community services and economic development through a community survey which formed the basis of a strategic plan for the area. From this survey, a tri-fold handout was developed and distributed including a community map with history and locations of craft shops, accommodations, stores, hiking trails, fishing rivers, church services and special events to advertise the area.

My presence in the community was for the most part warmly accepted through attendance at social activities including cribbage on Monday night, frequent community and church hall potluck suppers, lobster suppers, flea markets and auctions. There were milling frolics and square dances along with plays put on by the St. Ann's Bay Players. I also took Gaelic classes and was invited to join the Gaelic choir which sang at Sunday church services and community concerts.

No matter how much I engaged, my acceptance was still influenced by the attention that came from the public notoriety and the rumor mill stories following my exposure of government corruption. Private encouragement, support and friendship did not always bring public endorsement.

For example, I had taken a palliative care course with the intent of volunteering to support those going through the lonely process of transition from this life to the next. However, upon completing the course the director of the hospice society said that because of my public persona my acceptance as a volunteer was not welcome as it may upset some family members with loved ones near the end of life.

On a five-year trial basis, the United and Presbyterian churches had come together to offer a joint ministry to their respective dwindling congregations under the stewardship of a Baptist minister. I was a member of this community and attended the Sunday service, singing in the choir and helping out with Sunday school for the children culminating in the writing and directing of a Christmas Cantata.

For the weeks prior to Christmas, the children rehearsed their lines, parents fashioned costumes, props were made to be placed on the altar and the choir practiced their hymns to perfection. The pageant came together magically with the congregation silently attentive to each scene as it unfolded.

In the new year at my first and only attendance at a church sponsored bible study the minister read a passage and invited the group to give their thoughts as to the meaning. The group was very attentive to my insights, and this opened up a deeper dialogue which triggered the minister who went into a rage.

I was accused of being of the devil, kicked out of the class, and told never to come back. Obviously, my presence upset him, and I don't think my biblical interpretation bothered him as much as the interest and attention that I was receiving from his congregation. Not only was bible study over for me, but he also made it clear that my Sunday school volunteer services was no longer welcome. This pretty well ended my involvement with his ministry.

There was a real need in the community to provide for seniors, especially those widowed and living alone. Using my engineering and design management background, a plan was developed to repurpose a vacant elementary school building in North River Bridge to be used as a senior's assisted living facility.

Each classroom would be converted into a bed sitting room containing a kitchenette, bathroom, sleeping, and living area, each with direct access to an outside patio. Common services included kitchen, dining, laundry, and social area with a combination of staff and volunteers providing the housekeeping and cooking support.

The plan was well received and endorsed by the community, and it was time to establish a committee to raise funds and turn the concept into reality. At this point, one of the community leaders with political connections came to me privately and told me that because my name was associated with the idea it would not receive provincial funding and be allowed to go forward.

I naively thought my role in exposing political corruption with a goal of bringing good government to the people of Nova Scotia would be appreciated. I now realize that nothing could be further from the truth and that I would have to pay dearly for upsetting the apple cart – the system would go to no ends to put me in my place.

Nevertheless, I did spend a number of months running the small local gas station in Indian Brook which, especially during the off season, was a popular morning drop in spot for the locals to catch up on news, have a coffee and top up with gas.

This was followed up with painting and other odd jobs such as shingling roofs and building stables for trail riding venture in North River Bridge which imported hardy Newfoundland ponies from that province.

A far cry from my days as a senior civil servant, but all part of the necessary journey to come to know myself. It was time to learn humility and over the next number of years the practical applications of that lesson would come into play.

It was also a time to learn acceptance and to go with the flow by focusing on what is in front of me and carrying out those activities with focused intention. Afterall, it wasn't what one does that is important, it is how one does what one does that counts.

Following your heart by doing things in a peaceful, loving, and considerate way, treating those you are interacting with in a kind considerate manner and treating them as extensions of yourself you both grow and evolve along the path.

On the day the ponies arrived, they were unloaded from a trailer to a fenced pasture following a ten-hour trip from Newfoundland across the ferry to North Sydney and then to their new home in North River Bridge.

Late that afternoon, I decided to saddle up one of the ponies and walked into the pasture with a lead which I attached to the pony's halter and as I did so the horse pulled to the left to avoid a kick from another horse who was running close by.

The move pulled me into the kick which landed full force between my pelvic bone and navel. Martial arts and other training over the years had blessed me with firm abdominal muscles which withstood the blow and I continued with my goal, saddled the horse, and took it for a ride to christen the new trail.

That night, the shock of the blow had left me immobile with pain. Even blinking was excruciating, and an ambulance was called the next morning to take me to the hospital in Baddeck for x-rays. The paramedics slid me onto a stiff plywood board and loaded me into the ambulance for the twenty-mile ride in which every bump in the road was felt. Somehow, I was able to get onto the x-ray table and luckily, no broken bones were found.

While waiting alone on the emergency room gurney I needed to relieve myself and using the motorized back rest was able to sit up slowly and carefully swing my legs over the side; stood up; and walked into the washroom. Thinking that wasn't so bad and with my mobility back and the pain subsiding, I returned to my cubicle, dressed, and checked myself out.

Some weeks later I mentioned the incident to a blacksmith who informed me that I was lucky to be alive. Had the horse's hoof hit the hip, pelvic bone, or sternum, a blow like the one described could easily have led to serious injury or death. My angels were with me again.

We were now living in a small formal chapel in Jersey Cove that we were able to acquire at affordable terms from a retired Presbyterian minister and his wife who had converted the building for use as a summer home. The main floor of the chapel had been subdivided into a living/dining area with a small study on the side which led to a set of stairs and two small bedrooms built into a shed dormer that ran along the south side of the roof. Behind the living area was a small kitchen and bathroom and a door to the back yard which had two outbuildings, one of which was used as a workshop and the other for storage.

With a grant from the Department of Housing that Alexandra was intitled to because of her disability, renovations were made to add a bedroom and a dining room in two small wings added on to the back end of the building; relocate the stairs and enlarge the bathroom to make it more accessible. The former living/dining space was converted to a gallery and the study to a used bookstore. Our private space was now toward the back while the public gallery and used bookroom were at the front.

The Chapel Gallery of Fine Arts thus came into being, which afforded the opportunity of making supplementary income during the tourist season by showcasing the talented artists and artisans of the area to the visitors of the world-famous Cabot Trail. Art works were brought in on a consignment basis and other Cape Breton souvenir gifts and cards bought wholesale for retail sales. The used bookstore functioning as a book exchange was popular with tourists and locals alike and our inventory was never depleted.

Our new home was a place of mystical encounters. One evening shortly after moving in while sitting alone on the couch meditating, I opened my eyes to see three aliens standing in front of me. They appeared to be in holographic form and could best be described as human-like with small bodies, smooth, grey-colored skin; enlarged, hairless heads; and large, black eyes. My thought at the time was that they were a family with a tall father, medium height mother and a smaller child who were simply looking at me. I cannot say that a message was given, or if there was, that the download was consciously received. Their appearance did not startle me because the acceptance of life from other planets and visitations to earth was to those who cared to investigate the phenomena well documented and has been part of this reality for eons of time.

On another occasion while working in the garden a white dove flew in and landed close by staying with me for a time before flying away. This was followed weeks later while walking on popular hiking trail with a friend, a shiver was felt along my right side and at that moment my friend turned and saw a leprechaun holding my hand.

Maintaining a connection to my angels, and guides and a relationship with the "All That Is" is of paramount importance to me and there is nothing that could move me away from the source of my being through whom I lived in peace and harmony.

In the early years together, Alexandra kept involved with her psychic gifts, doing her weekly dream interpretation column, doing tarot readings for clients by appointment and at psychic fairs from Sydney to Yarmouth. Together we conducted past life regressions for individuals to help them understand the meaning and purpose of this life and the influences that past lives may have with current life challenges and lessons. Similarly, we worked on helping lost souls in move on after they had died.

Helping lost souls who had not realized that they had died find the light and move on to the next life was an activity that gave me great satisfaction. A lost or confused soul would come to us through Alexanda and want to communicate. I would speak to them asking their name and have them look around and let me know where they were and what they were doing. The stories are countless, from individuals who were intoxicated and had been in a severe car accident to those who have taken their own life with no belief in an afterlife and found themselves in a dark fog. The first order of business was for them to accept the fact that they had died and then guide them to look and listen intently for a source of light or sound no matter how dim or faint it may be and lead them to it. The closer they got to the source of the light or sound, the nearer they were to meeting up with and embracing their guides and loved ones who were waiting to lead them across the threshold. My departing message to go along and see what awaits was always accepted with heartfelt appreciation from the soul completing this important step in their transition between one life and another.

I had come to the realization that the battles fought were taking place on not only the physical plane but in the spiritual planes as well - 'As above, so below' - and that physical manifestations have a metaphysical component.

In the duality of this third dimensional plane of existence equal and opposite forces present choices for our attention. The tests, trials, and tribulations of our divinely given free will strengthen us as we learn through experience that following the example of Jesus and going within for guidance, we can overcome any adversity.

I clearly remember one-night wrestling all night long with a dark entity who was trying to possess Alexandra as she slept and thinking that if the dark side could not influence me directly, they would send their minion to influence me indirectly through someone close to me.

Perhaps this was a premonition as shortly afterward, Alexandra went from using a cane to a walker and then to a wheelchair, I realized that her MS was getting progressively worse and because she needed permanent care it was necessary to stay close to home to look after her. In a few short months Alexandra was for all intents and purposes bedridden with home care coming in once a day to provide support and give me some respite time.

The off-season income from the Gallery was nonexistent and there were times that the only traffic on the road was from the half dozen or so neighbors and the winter months became very desolate.

These quiet times afforded me the opportunity to pursue my metaphysical interests in an effort to come to know myself. A countless number of books and articles had significant impact in this regard which reintroduced me to timeless universal concepts and ideas which were new to me in this life. Over the next few years some of the more notable concepts came through off world or channeled information which by now had become very familiar to me.

The early days were focused on the Seth Material channeled by Jane Roberts in which she communicated information on the nature of reality from a nonphysical entity who identified himself as Seth.

The core teachings of the Seth Material are based on the principle that consciousness creates matter, and that each of us creates our own reality through the inputs of our thoughts, beliefs, and expectations. On a moment-by-moment basis referred to as the "point of power" we can affect change in our lives to get an alternate outcome by making adjustments to these inputs. The cause-and-effect relationship between our thoughts and reality are ours to explore through our free will and free choice and all experiences are valid.

According to Seth, between lives we planned the experiences and lessons to be learned in the upcoming life and established agreements with other souls to assist each other on our life's chosen path in a reciprocal way. This plan referred to as our probable reality has the potential to deviate from the plan and at each major choice point alternate or possible realties can present themselves that result in the necessity of making course adjustments if we choose to get back to our original plan. These possible realities live themselves out by aspects of our multidimensional selves in parallel universes and timelines that we are connected to. When one sees visons through their imagination as to what would have happened if I chose "this" instead of "that" they are tapping into a parallel life that plays out the alternate choice.

I deeply resonated with the work of Barbara Marciniak who through channeling our future selves from the Pleiades star cluster in her book Bringers of the Dawn. The Pleiadeans are advanced beings with an interest in assisting humanity with the evolution of consciousness to awaken us to our 'GOD' given potential. Many Pleiadeans such as Barbara have incarnated at this time as Starseeds who work through their home planet and other interdimensional star systems to impart knowledge and information to help us discover how to reach a new stage of evolution as we move into the Aquarian Age. Their guidance takes us way from obedience to the controlling structures and domination by others including governmental and religious authorities as programmed through the propaganda of mass media and their mission is to awaken humanity to their GOD given sovereignty. Individual freedom and responsibility can be achieved through the quest for truth by exploring multiple points of view and through mastering discernment come to our own truth. Most importantly we are to keep an open and flexible mind. The channeling guides us to move beyond our fears to reclaim the magnificence of our origins as humans and reminds us that we as part of the family of light and share an ancient ancestry with the universe around us.

Although not necessarily channeled information, I gravitated to the inspired work of Marilyn Ferguson "The Aquarian Conspiracy" in which she describes human potential for a new consciousness revolution bringing about a paradigm shift in modern culture leading to social change evolving from the personal transformation of individuals in all walks of life. She was at the forefront of describing a way of living more guided by personal motivation and less by dogma and hierarchical structure in which our evolution is supported as we go with the flow and not decreed through the hierarchical structures which currently dominates our lives.

Another intellectual that influenced my thinking at the time was Gary Zukav with his books The Dancing Wu Li Masters in which he explored the relationship between the quantum phenomena of modern physics and metaphysical concepts opening to theories related to the ultimate nature of our universe.

In the Seat of the Soul, Zukav goes beyond the physical manifestation and interactions of matter and energy to the evolution of consciousness and the connectedness through our heart center to the collective consciousness making up all that there is. His works aligned with my thinking and reinforced my personal concepts that were evolving on the dual nature of man.

This dual nature of man concept postulates that man has his human nature, and his divine nature. Our human nature with its masculine emphasis is controlled by our ego and is focused on our place in the external world of materiality. Our left mind and mental faculties of reason and logic dominate our human nature and we tend to categorize people, circumstances, and events as to what is beneficial and what is not to insure our survival. Our masculine tendencies including survival of the fittest, competitiveness, winning, striving for supremacy, staying on top, maintaining control and dominance are all motivations of our human nature which have governed our way of being for millennia.

Alternatively, our divine nature with the heart at the center of our being is in touch with spiritual motivations and principles. Through heartfelt emotions of love, care, compassion, communication, cooperation, and concern for others we can be guided on a more conscious collaboration with others for the collective good of all. Messages come to us by way of the heart through inspiration, intuition and feelings and we must learn to develop this connection by going within. As we do so we re-awaken a relationship with our guides, angels and other etheric multi-dimensional beings who are with us to guide us as we move through the lessons chosen for our life's journey.

For too long our feminine nurturing inner divine nature has taken a back seat to the dominance of our masculine outwardly focused human nature and ego and we must come to learn to bring balance to our being by acknowledging both and bringing balance to both the divine masculine and divine feminine aspects within us. This can be done by accessing through our heart our divine nature to guide and inspire us as to what to do and then using our human nature and logic as accessed through our mind to work out the details of how to do it.

Life is a balance of dualities in this material plane of existence, and we can no longer succeed by suppressing our ego and living solely in an inner world of dreams and fantasies than we can by suppressing our divine guidance and not doing the footwork that manifests our creativity and brings joy and purpose to our life. The spiritual integration of a masculine oriented technological society with feminine oriented spiritual interests will lead to a more balanced, harmonious, and fulfilling world. We must learn through practice to integrate spiritual alignment and involvement in our day-to-day physical activities.

In practicing patience, I learned that it was easy to be calm and peaceful when everything was going as planned but much more challenging when things were not. I rely on my dreams, meditations, along with daily journaling to keep in touch and guide me in all that I do with a stoic outlook reinforced through inspiration, intuition and paying attention to synchronicity.

I know when I am on the right track when things fall into place and when they are not to reassess the situation ... as with the attempts to reconnect with the boys ... and let things go. As Kipling reminded me 'If you can meet with triumph and disaster and treat those two imposters just the same.'

In addition, to my spiritual studies, an interest in energy healing was pursued in more detail through a variety of methods most of which dealt with acting as a conduit to direct the flow of healing energy using the power of the mind through visualization; or clearing blockages in life force energy through reflexology and pendulum work.

My visualization techniques were patterned on the remote healing work of Edgar Cayce and the belief in the idea that our DNA are quantum particles that are connected through the collective consciousness field with other individuated units of consciousness (other people). Visualizing the etheric body of the person to be healed and projecting healing energy to the areas needing attention could be helpful.

In pendulum work connection to inner guidance or intuition is received and answers provided through the motion of the pendulum. I used a quartz crystal and could not only get responses to yes/no questions by the axis along which the pendulum moved but also increase or decrease the flow of energy depending on the clockwise or counterclockwise rotation of the pendulum. This was most helpful in balancing chakras, the energy vortices located in the body from the base of the spine to the top of the head.

Another common techniques for tapping into inner wisdom was muscle testing to determine if something is beneficial or harmful to your body. Here I would hold a substance in one hand and with the other hand attempt to snap my fingers.

If my thumb and middle finger snapped, the energy field given off by the substance would be incompatible with my energy field; conversely if the connection between my thumb and middle finger was strong and not easily moved the energy field was compatible and the substance beneficial. Over time muscle testing and variations of it that I learned to do individually was incorporated into my daily life. For me it was a simple and convenient way of tapping into guidance.

This interest in energy healing and unseen vibrations and other phenomena that could influence the body's health and wellbeing eventually led me to the study of reflexology and taking an online course on the subject. After weeks of study and digesting a series of books on the subject in preparation for a challenging open book exam, I passed with top marks which inspired me to offer treatment in the community as a way to obtain additional supplementary income. Eventually I went on to do more study and became a member of the Reflexology Association of Canada.

CHAPTER 19

Change In Fortune

My simple daily routines came to an abrupt end in mid-December 1997 when I received a call from my sister telling me that our mother had died of a massive heart attack. She had been at home and was doing her Christmas baking and had a tray of her famous 'Pigs In A Blanket' in the oven, stepped into her bedroom and collapsed. My brother Jimmy was visiting at the time and was unable to revive her and called 911. Agnes Francis Zareski, mother of fourteen was announced dead on arrival at the hospital.

Immediately arrangements were made to have someone stay with Alexandra, and I headed off to Chezzetcook to be with the family, many of whom had not spoken to me in years and considered me a persona non grata. Nevertheless, I had a right to be there and share my grief and condolences for a mother that I loved dearly.

I was after all her first-born son and carried nothing but good childhood memories for a mother who watched over and cared for each and every one of us equally. She was a remarkable woman who took life in stride and faced what it had to offer with dignity and grace and mostly on her own as my father was away from home for months at a time with the Canadian Navy.

As an example of her strength and organizational ability she undertook the packing and travel arrangement to take her young family of seven children across the Atlantic Ocean on a Cunard Liner in the middle of winter to set up home in Southsea England where my father was stationed in nearby Portsmouth for two-year of submariner training with the Royal Navy. She coordinated the return trip home two years later, now with nine children and again under rough and stormy north Atlantic seas. On disembarking at Halifax, two new daughters were introduced for the first time, as she had up until then told her mother and family nothing of the pregnancies or births.

At the packed funeral home, I was sitting with some of my sisters who had stayed closed to me through the years and shared a vision of my mother laying on a stone plinth draped with a white linen and seven ethereal beings or angels ministering to and protecting her. I received the message that her death was a shock to her and that she is still asleep and that the angels will stay with her and watch out for her until she awakens and can complete her journey to the other side.

After the visitation, the family and close friends gathered at my mother's home. I was sitting on one of the dining room chairs placed along the outside wall when Patricia and my two boys arrived. The room was packed as all eyes were on her as she came over to sit next to me and offer her deep felt condolences.

To her credit she stayed and chatted with me for few moments, and this broke the ice for Joseph and Tony, neither of whom I had had much contact with for several years to come over and join me. As we hugged and talked, as far as I was concerned, there was no one else in the room other than the three of us.

My joy was overwhelming as the boys opened up and filled me in with what was happening in their lives. This reunion was to me a silver lining in the unexpected loss of my mother who at another level used her passing to reconnect me with my boys and family. It was a glorious reunion in an otherwise sorrow-filled event.

The funeral was held at St. Geneivieve's in East Chezzetcook. The day was cloudy and overcast as the family walked to the reserved pews at the front of a packed church. My two older sisters, Shelly and Terry were on each elbow as we made our way to our seat directly in front and to the right of the altar.

While standing in our place still arm in arm the clouds broke and a beam of light came through an upper window of the church and shone like a spotlight directly on me. I immediately began sobbing deeply, my knees became weak, and I was about to fall but luckily was propped up by my sisters at either side until I recovered my composure, and it was time to be seated.

Later in the mass, while the priest was holding up the host and reciting the eucharistic prayer, I could clearly see Jesus in full form hovering behind and slightly above the priest with his arm stretched out to the side looking directly at me saying. "Everything is going to be all right."

Afterward, at the reception in the church hall, all who I spoke to shared glowing and wonderful memories of my mother which only reinforced the tremendous regard in which all that came to know her magnanimous spirit felt for her. One friend, having met up with my mother only a few days before her passing recounted how radiant she looked and felt that it was my mother's way of saying goodbye. While another told the story of my mother being there for her in a moment of need with no questions asked or expectation in return.

The ripple effect of the love, compassion and kindness of this remarkable women affected the lives of countless numbers of people and is still evident today through her children and grandchildren as they carry on her legacy.

One of the most pleasant surprises following my return to Jersey Cove and a memory that I will always cherish was an unexpected visit the next summer by Joseph and his girlfriend Emma who were touring the scenic Cabot Trail.

The day was magical as we drove to Ingonish and took in the spectacular views from the top of Cape Smokey and the sights of the Ingonish area. On the way back we stopped for gas at the Wreck Cove General Store run by a friend who graciously set the young couple up with a late afternoon sea kayak excursion in the waters off the foot of Smokey.

That evening we enjoyed a huge bonfire on the beach, the hours passed too quickly while catching up with Joseph and connecting with his partner to be. Before we knew it stars in the night sky were shining brightly over us as if they wanted to participate in our happy reunion and let us know that we would continue to maintain this connection built on love no matter what lay ahead.

In the weeks after my mother's funeral, I realized that life as a caretaker supported by welfare and a meagre disability pension for Alexandra could be received closer to Halifax/Dartmouth if only we had a place to stay. Furthermore, I realized that meaningful year-round employment was not available from a base in Jersey Cove and the local economy. It was my hope that with the passing of time old wounds may have healed and more employment opportunities would open up in my engineering profession if I moved back home.

I shared the idea of moving back with my sister Mary and she introduced me to an opportunity of acting as a caretake for a cottage belonging to an acquaintance of hers who worked away in Bermuda and whose husband was at sea for months at a time with the merchant marine. The circumstances could not have worked out better and in the late summer of 1998 we packed what we could in a small trailer and were on our way to live on Porter's Lake halfway between my family's home base in Chezzetcook and the twin cities of Halifax/Dartmouth. The property owners had no objections to me making modifications to accommodate Alexandra's wheelchair accessibility needs or any other improvements I wanted to make to the property. It was a win-win for both sides; upgrades, maintenance, and repairs both inside and out in exchange for a place to stay.

In order to transfer the government support payments to this new jurisdiction it was necessary to complete several application forms and show that I was looking for work. With no work on the horizon, community services suggested I take a home care course and perhaps find employment in that field, which given my background and experience was hard to accept as a serious and viable option for me. Eventually my caretaker allowance was continued as there was no other option available to us at the time.

Alexandra's condition slowly deteriorated even more and she needed constant care and attention. Even leaving the house for an hour or so to pick up groceries or do the laundry could result in finding Alexandra lying on the floor and unable to get up and those not knowing the circumstances felt she was not being properly looked after. To receive the appropriate level of home care, Alexandra had to be assessed by a home care nurse who on the completion of her visit told me that the living arrangement for Alexandra was not sustainable, and that Alexandra needed more care than I was capable of providing.

Following that assessment, a director in the provincial social services department who quite frankly told me that not only Alexandra's health was at stake but mine was as well and that if Alexandra was single a nursing home bed could be found for her right way but as long as we were married, I would be expected to look after her on my own.

After more than seven years as the sole personal care provider looking after all of Alexandra's needs to maintain her activities of daily living, I had to admit that slowly but surely, my once vibrant strength and vitality were slipping away. With no light at the end of the tunnel we mutually agreed to file for an uncontested divorce which triggered Alexandra being in line to receive the full-time care she needed once a bed became available for her.

The granting of the official divorce decree and the placement for a temporary nursing home bed for Alexandra came at almost the same time. One afternoon the respite care worker arrived to give me a break and upon my return, later in the day, Alexandra was gone. In a follow-up call with Social Services, I was told that Alexandra was on her way to a homecare facility and as per her request the location would not be revealed to me. Our lives from that point on went in different directions.

I will be forever grateful for the time spent with Alexandra and her love and support in giving me a safe haven during my trials and tribulations with the government and guidance in coming to understand the deeper levels of my spirituality and metaphysical abilities. She was there to encourage my Rosicrucian studies, introduced me to my spirit guides and higher self, helped me understand the dream world and to become a channel for the higher dimensions. There is no doubt in my mind that there was a karmic bond between us that we agreed to work out in our time together.

My interest in energy healing led to contact with a small group in a private residence where one of the participants was Gail Slater with whom I felt a deep familiarity. When the introductions were made, I spontaneously held both of her hands in mine and told her she had good energy. From that moment Gail became part of my life. She was a kind, considerate, compassionate, and sensitive soul who was the focal point of the meditation group.

Our time together was magical. On one occasion we were on a short-day trip and stopped by a fish and chips shop to get lunch. The proprietor when seeing us said that as a couple we glowed and gave us our meals at no charge. At other times we could see the true essence of individuals we were talking to as their faces and countenance would transform before our very eyes. It was as if we could see into their souls.

There were other strange and unexplained events that happened to us in those early days as if the dark forces did not want us to get together. One morning while driving into the city the car steering wheel was pulling me into the ditch and it was all I could do to keep the car on the road to avoid a serious accident. On another occasion while visiting Gail at her second story flat we watched the bathtub on the spur-of-the-moment fill up through the open drain with dirty dark water and sludge before just as quickly being emptied away. This was followed days later by a potted plant that started to spontaneously combust that we had to extinguish in the kitchen sink. Both of us, having a strong sense of and connection to the spiritual realms took such incidents in stride and called on our guides to protect us within a radiant sphere of white light.

For practicality Gail gave up her flat and moved in with me to the cottage on Porter's Lake. It was quite an adjustment for her, from having been living alone for the last ten years to sharing her life again with another but it proved to be the right thing for both of us, and the doors of opportunity began to open.

The wooded area on the property needed to be thinned out and there were gardens to be built and maintained along with a shoreline with the dilapidated wharf and the potential for a nice sandy beach if the rocks and boulders we're moved around. This was my physical activity for that summer, and I spent everyday rain or shine doing something or other outside including time spent either moving rocks or swimming in the brackish waters of Porters Lake.

In a short time, we had a large fire pit, a rock wall on the shoreline, a stable secure wharf, and a nice sandy beach for the younger guests to swim from. There were times that I would dive under the water to move a large boulder out of the way and Gail would wonder if I would ever be coming up for air. The physical activity was good for my body and soul and my vibrant health and vitality quickly returned.

Gail was a young mother to a daughter Wendy who in her own right became a young mother to a daughter Meghann. As a young woman growing up Wendy loved life and as the nucleus of friends, family, and schoolmates her light of inspiration shone brightly through her academic achievements and participation in figure skating, horseback riding, modeling, and artistic endeavors.

Later as a young mother herself, Wendy began her struggles with addiction and mental illness and knowing that she could not properly care for her daughter abandoned her family disappearing for months at a time. Gail shared with me a lot of the heartbreak that she went through with Wendy and much of the hard road that Wendy traveled including homelessness, drug, and alcohol addiction. Through it all, Wendy and her mother maintained a bond with Gale being the touchstone that Wendy relied on.

When I first met Wendy, I thought to myself what a powerful soul she must be to choose this lifetime to experience what she is going through. I hold the belief that nothing in life is an accident and that each and every one of us as an individuated unit of Divine consciousness is doing exactly what we should be doing and that the trials and tribulations that we face strengthen us and expands our experience as a soul.

Consequently, I vowed to myself to support Gail in her effort to ensure that Wendy was safe, had a roof over her head and food on her table no matter what. I was blessed to be in Wendy's life and help her through this long and arduous journey that she had embarked upon. Knowing that the most powerful and healing force in the universe is love, my love and support was there for Wendy and her mother.

One weekend Wendy came to visit us in Porters Lake. At that time, I was doing reflexology sessions for a few clients and offered Wendy a treatment that she willingly accepted. While sitting in a comfortable chair with her foot on my lap the session was just starting when Wendy's demeanor changed in a flash. Her face took on an evil sinister appearance and in a deep raspy guttural voice said to me "She is mine. You can't have her."

I knew then that Wendy was dealing with a malevolent entity that was trying to scare me off, which did not work. In a calm measured voice, I looked Wendy directly in the eye and said, "I believe it's best that I take you home." At that moment, seeing that I was not afraid, the entity stepped back, and Wendy came forward as an obedient child expressed no objection was packed and ready to go early the next morning.

CHAPTER 20

Back in the Saddle

By chance while living in Porter's Lake I reconnected with my family doctor Mac Duncan and his wife who were now retired and invited us for supper to catch up.

When I was a student at St. Mary's University in Halifax, my roommate was babysitting their son Torquil which led to me to accompany my friend on his visits with the Duncan family. Soon I was a regular visitor, and their home became a welcome refuge from residence life at the university and we maintained a close family connection over the years, but I had not been in touch with him since the publicity around the Buchanan corruption accusations.

At our visit we spoke about my work prospects, and he mentioned that Torquil was managing a project in Poland where there was an opening for an engineer. He agreed to let him know of my availability and interest and over the next few weeks, interviews, application forms and other documents were finalized leading to my appointment.

The role was as a construction engineer for a joint project with the Saskatchewan Wheat Pool who were building a grain terminal facility in Gdansk Poland. The start date for my employment was continually postponed however in August a plane tickets came in the mail for a departure in mid-September which did not leave a lot of time to prepare.

The first order of business was to give up the living arrangement at Porter's Lake, which worked out well as the owners were planning to put the property on the market. We rented a small one bedroom in the south end of Halifax for Gail to stay in while I was gone.

The work/travel arrangements allowed for a two-week visit home for every three months working away or alternatively your partner's flight overseas for a visit would be paid for if you decided not to come home.

Arrangements were made with Gail's son to take care of our dog; visits to Cape Breton to share the news with Gails's parents and her daughter Wendy were made. My fiftieth birthday was celebrated with our children and their partners at a popular Italian Pizza restaurant and later my sister hosted a family bon-voyage barbeque at her home in Chezzetcook. It was interesting to me how life can change on a dime from being unemployed and cut off from friends and family for ten years to starting a new job in another country and being accepted back into the family fold.

Although my family's participation in the events of the past was never brought up, the impact on my life, although diminished over time, could never be completely forgotten. It was my nature to forgive but not forget, and there was still a private resolve on my part to tell my side of the story once the lifestyle previously enjoyed was re-established to some degree.

Although prospects were encouraging, we were still broke and needed some cash to pay the rent and other necessities in preparation for the trip. Unexpectedly an unsolicited credit card with a two-thousand-dollar limit arrived in the mail and we were on our way. It was synchronicity in action, our needs for financial resources were accommodated confirming we were on the right path.

On the day before the departure, we moved our possessions to the apartment and while I was setting things up Gail went back to the cottage to pick up the last few items including the telephone answering machine. Gail told me that there was a message on the machine from Torquil to call him back as the start date for my job in Poland had been postponed yet again.

I was faced with a dilemma, either call back and risk losing the job or ignore the last-minute message and fly to Poland the next morning. With bags packed and ticket in hand, I flew to Poland where I was met at the Gdansk Airport by Torquil; neither of us saying a word about the message. Upon arrival at the jobsite, office accommodations and other arrangements for me to work with were hastily being set up. It was evident that my visit was not expected, nevertheless, I was courteously received and would make the best of it.

The project site, on the shores of the Baltic Sea was located adjacent to the Westerplatte peninsula in the port of Gdansk where sixty years earlier on 1 September 1939 the Germans attacked a small Polish garrison marking the first battle and beginning of the Second World War. The job site also contained several reinforced concrete bunkers built by the German army along the shores of the Baltic to defend the occupied area from Allied attack by sea.

The project team was made up primarily of Canadian expatriates supplemented by a number of Polish engineers and support staff. While investors along with the company's senior management were negotiating financing and other high level business matters, the project was moving forward at a snail's pace.

This gave me time to hone my skills on the latest project software applications; to review in detail the work underway; and plan for the completion phases when funding became available. It felt good to get my technical engineering/management mind back to work and to be able to build on past years of experience in the design and construction industry.

That fall, rather than me taking a break to go home, Gail join me in Gdansk staying for a couple of months. We brought in the start of the new millennium with a New Years Eve celebration on the historic Dugas Street in Gdansk. My days were busy with work, however alone in a foreign country the long hours by herself were monotonous for Gail.

For variety we planned several weekend excursions to give us both something to look forward to. During our time in Poland, we took the company car and travelled throughout the region mostly alone but occasionally with another couple.

On one trip we toured Auschwitz and while walking down a stairwell Gail mentioned how realistic the experience was with the strong smell of chlorine. She was picking this up psychically as no one else in our group detected it. On a trip to Berlin, we visited the New Palace at Potsdam where Gail had a deja vu experience of having lived there in a past life. I had a similar experience while visiting the castle of the Teutonic Order of Knights in Malbork.

Our travels took us east to the Wolf's Lair, Hitler's first Eastern Front military headquarters in World War II and south to Zakopane a resort town at the base of the Tatras Mountains and then to nearby Kraków, a southern Poland city near the border of the Czech Republic, known for its well-preserved medieval core.

Our most memorable trip was a flight to Rome where we spent a week taking in all of the sights. When asked where we went and what we saw, we often referred to our weekend excursions as an "ABC" trip an acronym for a visit to - Another Bloody Castle or Church or Cathedral.

On 1 April 2000, while home on two weeks' leave, we tied the knot. There was a lot to do to get ready for the wedding, from setting up and moving to a new apartment, buying furniture, a car, and all the myriad other nuptial arrangements. On the day of the wedding furniture was being assembled and our apartment decorated before the evening ceremony attended by my boys Joe and Tony my best man and Gail's son David and granddaughter Meghann her maid of honor. The next day we drove to visit Gail's family in Cape Breton and the following day Gail drove me to the airport for another work term in Gdansk where she would join me for a visit later in the summer.

Over the next few months, the early phases of construction work that had approved funding in place had been completed and the project came to a virtual standstill. Time has a tendency to drag out when there is no activity to focus on and get your teeth into and those were the circumstances for all of us as we waited patiently for the funding to be sorted out. There was a team in place ready to go and we doubled down on planning, scheduling, for upcoming procurement activities for the completion phases of work.

While in Poland I was having a problem with a tooth ache which resulted in a visit to a dentist and an extraction. Days later, while walking across the site a feeling of weakness came over me and I fell to my knees. I got up and regained my composure and carried on, however over the next while the condition continued, and thinking it might be related to an infection from the tooth removal made an appointment with the company doctor to have a checkup. This resulted in admission to the hospital in Gdansk for a thorough observation and assessment including being hooked up to a halter monitor to check my heart function.

I was in a ward with four other men and noticed that their families were continually around looking after them, changing their bedding, cleaning, and feeding them. The reason became evident at suppertime when a large aluminum pot on casters was rolled up to my bed and a scoop of green slop was placed on a plate in front of me. Needless to say, when friends from the office called to ask if I needed anything my immediate response was a burger and fries.

While in the hospital the doctor came by one morning concerned that my heart rate was registering too low on the monitor and asked if I would take a walk and climb the stairs to get my pulse up.

I was discharged with no diagnosis as to what was causing the weakness spells, and this concerned me. Since there was not much happening on site, I asked for permission to go home to Canada to have a medical assessment carried out and again, a clean bill of health was received.

A couple of days prior to my scheduled return to Poland, Gail and I were walking along a beach, and I told her that I saw no point in returning. The project was at a standstill and the prospect of getting the necessary financing was not looking good. Torquil was not happy with my decision to leave the team, however in hindsight it was the right decision as a short time later the project was mothballed, never to be completed.

When one door closes, another door opens, and the new door was an advertisement in the newspaper looking for a construction engineer and a project accountant for a new hospital to be built in Summerside PEI.

I updated my resume and made application and in my covering letter, suggested that I was interested in both positions. Within a week or so I was invited to the offices of East Prince Partnership Ltd. (EPPL) for an interview. EPPL was a partnership between two of the largest general contractors in Prince Edward Island who had joined forces to win the contract to build a new regional hospital.

The interview went well and to my pleasant surprise, I was informed that they were not considering me for the positions that I applied for and asked if I would be willing to take on the role as Project Manager and asked if I could start right away.

Now after more than ten years of being blackballed in Nova Scotia and not able to use my engineering and management experience I was on the threshold of re-establishing my professional career and reputation back in Canada.

Gail was delighted with the news, and we gave up our apartment in Halifax and bought our first home in Summerside. Although we were not back in Nova Scotia, we were close enough to make regular visits and to host family and close friends while vacationing on the island and taking in summer fun and activities including the world famous all you can eat lobster suppers and the must-see Anne of Green Gables production at the Confederation Center in nearby Charlottetown.

The early weeks and months were very busy with mobilizing construction offices on site, commencing site work, while concurrently developing systems and procedures to manage all aspects of the work including scheduling, cost control, project, and contract administration to name but a few.

In addition, the project team made up of all new hires on both the construction and administrative side had to be guided and motivated to achieve the collaborative cohesive team chemistry necessary for success. The birthing pains experienced by EPPL in the first few weeks were successfully worked out and the $40 million hospital project went on to be completed on schedule and on budget.

As the project was wrapping up it was evident that a new assignment had to be found. EPPL had no upcoming work and an opportunity to move back to Nova Scotia came through the mechanical contractor Sayers and Associates with offices in Dartmouth who invited me to join them as a Project Manager.

It was interesting that in order to get work that had been denied for so long in my home province, I had to leave the country and come back after proving myself in another province. Had I not done so, it was extremely unlikely that I would have found work at home as a professional engineer.

With future work in place, we set up a home in Dartmouth and I commuted back and forth for a couple of months while wrapping up the Summerside project. My routine was to leave Summerside on mid Friday afternoon to spend the weekend at home and then leave Dartmouth at dawn on Monday mornings arriving at the job site for 9:00 am.

On one of these trips back to Summerside, I was up well before dawn, filled the company truck with gas, and headed on my way. At this time of the morning there was practically no traffic on the road, as I settled in for the three-and-a-half-hour drive.

My next recollection was the sound and jolt of a crash which shook me up. As I regained awareness of my surroundings, my vehicle was stopped only feet away from a heavy-duty traffic light pole on the opposite side of a major intersection. My lack of attention resulted in me running the traffic light and hitting a utility van broadside. The van ended up flipping over and landing on its roof. The driver of the van was fine with no injuries and although my airbag had not been deployed I as well had not a scratch on me. The front of my truck was smashed in like an accordion and I couldn't believe that both of us walked away unharmed. A split second before or after the van would have struck me on the driver's side or I would have stuck the light standard head on resulting in a much more serious outcome. It was not my time, and my angels were watching out for me yet again.

A short time later emergency vehicles and police were on site to clean up after the incident. The police officer recognizing me from the publicity surrounding my stand against the government ten years earlier offered to drive me home so that I could let Gail know what happened. He was kind enough to take me to a car rental agency where I picked up a vehicle to continue my journey. Weeks later, after the truck was repaired, it was given to me by EPPL as a bonus at the end of the project.

Sayers had offices in the Burnside Industrial Park and had several significant projects on the books that were assigned to me to manage. The transition into the company's culture didn't take long as I had been dealing with most of their management team over the last several months.

One morning, while discussing project financing details in the company accountant's office I blacked out and slid off of my chair onto the floor. As quickly as I lost consciousness, I regained it and suggested that there was nothing wrong and I'd be fine.

Not buying that, they called Gail and had me sent to the Dartmouth General Hospital for an assessment where Gail was awaiting my arrival. We were sitting quietly in the waiting room in the emergency department anticipating our turn and a slight fluttering feeling in my abdominal area turned into an uncontrolled shaking which took over my whole body. My next recollection was hearing Gail calling for help while my body was lying on the floor. This was the second time that I blacked out that morning and was immediately brought into a cubicle for observation.

By this this time I quickly regained my faculties but knew that I wasn't going to get out of there without a thorough examination. They put probes on my body to check my heart function and I was interviewed by an emergency room doctor who asked if I was an athlete because my resting pulse rate was in the low forties which was typically seen in professional athletes.

A short time later I was visited by a cardiac surgeon who explained that I operated with such a low heart rate that when it gets too low it loses the signal to beat, the adrenaline will kick in which causes me to vibrate and then blackout because the heart is not pumping enough oxygen to the brain.

He told me now that the blackouts have started, they will become more frequent. In order to control the heart function to prevent these blackouts, a pacemaker would be installed that would kick in and tell my heart to beat when it was getting to a low threshold. He explained that because of the unpredictability of these blackouts, they could for example happen while I was driving and cause a serious accident.

With that information I connected the dots on the incidents over the last three years going back to my time in Poland where a weakness would come over me and I would drop to my knees; the halter monitor in the hospital where I was asked to climb the stairs to get my heart rate up; and here at home the traffic accident on my way to the job site in Summerside. Without sharing my thoughts with the doctor, I now had a logical rationale for those events and knew that the accident with the truck was the result of a blackout - not an inattentive moment.

The surgeon shared that he himself has a pacemaker installed for exactly the same conditions and that he would be inserting the same model and electrical probes. The surgery was booked right away, and the device installed with a battery life of roughly ten years.

The low limit threshold was set at sixty beats a second, which was much too high for me as I was used to operating in the forties, so they agreed to set it at fifty. My only requirement was to come into the pacemaker clinic for an annual checkup to evaluate the heart rate data collected and determine the remaining life of the battery.

I carried on with my physical activities as if nothing happened and for the most part forgot that I had a pacemaker. The only precautions were when going through security scanning at airports or other such situation a physical pat down was needed. The technology is quite remarkable; they can monitor every beat of my heart and at my annual checkups would pinpoint dates and times that my heartbeat was irregular and ask for details on my activities at those times.

Shortly after my pacemaker was installed it was time to move on from Sayers and Associates. The major projects that I have been working on had come to an end and I was waiting around for something to seek my teeth sink into.

While working away at my cubicle one morning I noticed my brother David going into meet with the president of the company. He obviously knew that I was working there but did not inform me of his intended visit or afterward why he was there. My only speculation was that he was checking up on me. I said nothing to David, and he said nothing to me, nevertheless I was suspicious of his motives.

While at Sayers, I completed extracurricular studies with the Project Management Institute and obtained the Project Management Professional (PMP) designation and went out on my own with Zareski Associates Project Managers (ZAPM). I did a number of small jobs for a variety of clients and was building a reputation albeit slowly under the circumstances of still not being welcome by the government and major clients with strong government connections.

My work tended to be with private sector and interestingly enough a couple of those came about through my brother David again. One was a major condominium project and the other a private surgical clinic in Dartmouth.

As one of my projects was coming to an end and another just starting in the preliminary planning stages I received a call from a headhunter from

Vancouver asking if I would give a reference to a fellow engineer that I had worked with in Poland.

My former colleague was given a favorable reference and the recruiter then asked what I was doing. After giving him some details, he asked if I would consider coming to Vancouver for an interview with BC Hydro who were looking for people of my background and experience.

A week later I was being interviewed by officials at BC Hydro's engineering office in Burnaby and was offered the position of Construction Manager for their Hydro Spillway Gate Reliability Program. This project involved the upgrading of the spillway gates and related dam safety infrastructure at the twenty-two dam sites across British Columbia.

BC Hydro was not at all concerned with my lack of previous experience in the hydro electric utility business, they were interested in my project management credentials; the details of the hydro business would sort themselves out.

I agreed to the position and would be starting work two weeks later as a consultant to BC Hydro through the head-hunting company. The details fell into place as if they had been planned for some time. With our house on the market and furniture in storage Gail and I were off on another adventure.

Initially we stayed in an apartment in Vancouver's Coal Habour neighborhood with a stunning view of West Vancouver and the Coast Mountains beyond and eventually settled into a townhouse in Burnaby a five-minute walk from the office.

My work with BC Hydro went extremely well and was very satisfying. I oversaw the construction of major upgrades to a number of dam sites. The scope of work varied on a site-by-site basis and was implemented in a prioritized manner. This was important work; a failure at a dam could cause catastrophic flooding and take out communities on the downstream side.

Through my work on this program, I was able to introduce a newly evolving surveying technology that uses laser light to capture 'point clouds' of data giving extremely precise measurements of existing site conditions which could be converted to three-dimensional drawings. This technology saved weeks of work and gave a much more accurate profile of existing spillway structures in order to plan and implement the critical restorations and repair work.

In the course of my work, I interacted with a number of program managers within BC Hydro and was called upon to carry out other functions including managing the upgrades to the gantry cranes in the power plants around the province as well as the emergency backup diesel generating power systems in remote locations.

My plate was full, and I enjoyed the challenges that the work presented and before long I was looked upon as the go-to-guy to get things done. With my current projects progressing smoothly I was invited to join the newly formed Mica 5 and 6 team to plan all aspects of the eight hundred-million-dollar project.

The Mica generating station located 145 kilometers north of Revelstoke on the Columbia River, was built within a mountain and originally designed to house six generating units though only four were installed when the power plant was commissioned in the late 1970. The Mica 5 and 6 Project involved the installation of the two new 500 megawatt generating units into the remaining two empty bays at the far end of the powerhouse.

As construction manager in the planning stages I was responsible for establishing the work breakdown structure and flow for the installation of the new turbine generators and supporting infrastructure. An initial assignment was to establish the high-level implementation schedule identifying sequence of work and associated procurement activities for the relevant work packages while keeping the existing generator units fully functioning throughout the construction period. The presentation was successfully defended at a meeting of both senior BC Hydro officials and suppliers of turbines and generators interested in bidding on the work and established the contractual milestones for the project.

My work also included the planning and oversight of major infrastructure upgrades to BC Hydro's Mica Village about ten kilometers from the dam site where operations staff would be supplemented by an influx of visiting engineering staff from the head office.

Following that assignment, I was tasked with managing the design – build - operate proposal call and eventual delivery of the 400-bed construction campsite to house the temporary construction workers.

With the work packages clearly delineated it was necessary to meet with representatives of the construction trades unions to negotiate the extent of the work that would be carried out by BC Hydro's own forces versus the trade unions and also include provisions for participation of First Nations indigenous communities in the project.

Prior to the start of the meeting, the BC Hydro senior managers responsible for the project were unavailable and rather than rescheduling I presented the details of the project to the business agents who had travelled to Burnaby to attend.

My strategy was to agree on the non-contentious items and park the contentious items for later discussion. The most contentious being the construction and operation of the work camp which was claimed by the unions as their work. There was agreement on hundreds of millions of dollars of work for the unions and I wanted a fair share for the First Nations.

We finally agreed that the camp would be built to the specifications established by trade unions and that the first nations would be involved in the building and operation of the facility. With that, a draft Memorandum of Understanding (MOU)was successfully negotiated and subsequently endorsed by senior management of BC Hydro, the trade unions, and the First Nations community, and this established the bases upon which the Mica project work would be completed.

The contract to install and operate the expanded camp facilities won by Horizon North Camps and Catering Partnership, a joint venture with the Neskonlith, Splatsin, and Adams Lake bands was at the time the largest tendered contracts ever awarded by BC Hydro to a First Nations joint venture.

Another challenging assignment related to the expansion of the powerhouse generating capacity was the Switchgear Replacement Project which included the extension of the switchgear building, along with improvements to the lead shafts and transformer galleries.

In order to meet the scheduled delivery dates for the switchgear equipment we were given a one-year time frame from start to finish to design and build the extension of the switchgear building. I worked closely with the private sector civil design engineers and came up with a timeline and solution that fast tracked the work to meet the fixed completion schedule. Even though the work was carried out through extreme winter conditions with 16-to-20-foot annual snowfalls, the job was completed on time.

Life in British Columbia was rewarding and full of activities. While there we travelled a lot; made lifelong friends; and reconnected with our extended families. I had cousins on my father's side who lived nearby and an aunt who lived in Victoria while Gail had a son in Calgary all of whom we regularly visited; but it was not the same as being home.

While we were away one of my seven sisters died of cancer and we flew home to attend her funeral. No sooner did we get back to British Columbia when we were travelling home again as news was received that another sister had died only two weeks later of the same horrible disease.

We found ourselves more than ever missing our families. Our hearts were home in Nova Scotia where my son's family was growing with the addition of two more grandchildren born while we were away, and where Gail's daughter and her welfare was an ongoing concern. With our minds made up we returned home in December 2010.

In the early days I continued to travel back and forth to the west coast to manage the completion and turnover of the BC Hydro projects and then took on assignments to work on the design and construction of multi-unit residential buildings in the Halifax area.

While living out west, Gail and I were patients of a licensed practitioner of Traditional Chinese Medicine who had recently moved to Vancouver from Guatemala. Over time we realized that we had a lot in common and became close friends with the doctor and his young family who became a surrogate family for us. We enjoyed each other's social company and introduced them to a Canadian Thanksgiving dinner with all of the fixing and they would reciprocate with traditional Guatemalan meals; a blend of Mayan culture with a touch of Spanish influence. Longing for home, the family made the long road trip back to their roots in Guatemala and perhaps this had motivated us to do the same.

Several months after we had moved back to Dartmouth and about two years after we had last heard from our Guatemalan friends, they contacted us a few days before Christmas in 2013 asking for a favor. Their infant daughter had been suffering from seizures and there was nothing that either traditional Chinese medicine or the modern western medical community could do for her. Her father contacted a local shaman who by using shamanistic practices was able to clear the negative energy from the auric field of the child that was causing the seizures and a full healing was achieved.

Our friends asked the Shaman who facilitated the healing what they could do to pay for the service provided and were told that they as a couple had untapped healing abilities and were required to take training to become shaman again in this life and share these spiritual healing gifts with others.

After two years of study, it was time for their formal initiation ceremony into the Mayan shaman community. As a couple, they were required to have a Shaman couple stand as godparents to present the initiates and vouch for them during the ceremony. The child's mother, claiming that we were the most spiritual couple she knew, insisted that our names be put forward even though we were not Shaman. A meeting of the shaman council was convened to consider the unorthodox request, and approval was granted to the initiates to have us stand with them. Gail and I agreed without question and now were faced with the problem that the ceremony was to be held on Christmas Eve, giving us only five days to make travel arrangements at this very busy time of year.

Everything miraculously fell into place, and we were on our way; an indication that this was something that we were meant to do. We ran into challenges as the flights were delayed due to bad weather conditions at Chicago and we were late getting into Dallas which caused us to miss our connecting flight to Guatemala City; the next day we were on our way again.

Upon arrival at our destination, our friend was there to meet us, but our luggage was not. This inconvenience resulted in us wearing the clothes on our back supplemented by a few local purchases until our bags were finally delivered a day before our return home. We stayed overnight in a tourist hotel in Guatemala City and were on the road early the next morning. It was a four-hour drive to their home in the western highlands just outside the city of Quetzaltenango, known locally by its Mayan name

Xela. The family had recently moved into a large new home that was designed and built to easily accommodate their five children.

The day before the ceremony, my friend took me to the Minerva Market in the northwest end of the city to pick up specific supplies from a list provided by the Mayan elders. As we were leaving, he led the way through the crowded maze of stalls, and I could see ahead that we were coming to a congested intersection where two main walkways crossed each other. With each arm laden with parcels, I jostled through the crowd and made my way out to the sidewalk. Arriving home, I realized that my wallet was missing and mentally retracing my steps accepted that I was jostled on purpose by a master pick pocket team who had set up the unsuspecting gringo as soon as they laid eyes on me. Fortunately, I was only carrying a small amount of cash and a credit card with me at the time. Accepting the incident as "meant to be" my approach in such circumstances is to accept what is and move on while mentally sending a blessing to the family for their masterful and creative procurement activities.

On the morning of the ceremony with supplies in hand we left before dawn to help set up, with the women and other relatives arriving later. The site of the ceremony was in a secluded wooded area in the very mystical Laguna de Ayaza region of Guatemala surrounded by several active volcanoes.

Gail and I were under the impression that the initiation ritual which started early in the morning would last an hour or so and that our role was simply to be there to support the couple during the ceremony much in the same way that a godparent would support and stand for a child being baptized. It turned out that we were wrong on both counts. The ceremony was an all-day event, and we were active participants involved with every aspects of the of the initiation from beginning to the end with our friends translating and guiding us through what to do and when to do it. This involved chanting, reciting prayers, dancing around a large fire to which we added incense and other offerings. It was a magical, mystical experience that flew by quickly for us as if we were in another dimension, and perhaps we were, and at some level perhaps we were being initiated along with our friends.

The ceremony concluded when our friends were presented with their leather medicine bags containing peppers, cacao, tobacco, and other traditional healing herbs. Afterwards, the chief Shaman thanked both Gail and I for our participation and presented us with a book on Mayan Shamanism. He introduced me as the 'Spirit of the East' and asked me to say a few words to those in attendance. He then went on to tell Gail that her totem was an eagle and that she flew close to God, and that my totem was a shark, a symbol of power, strength, and tenacity to never give up driving away negativity.

On the morning of our departure, we sat with the five children in the living room of their home and presented to them the Christmas gifts that had just arrived in our luggage. They were perfect angels sitting on the coach in front of us and so appreciative of these small tokens. Afterward, their parents shared with us that each child received a gift that perfectly suited their interest and personality. There is no doubt that even the small not so significant events in our lives are guided and do have an impact.

Our flight from Guatemala City was early in the morning so we decided to leave the day before and stay and the Holiday Inn to rest up before our journey. We left early enough to have lunch at a roadside restaurant and visit the ancient Mayan ruins of Iximche. This is the site that a few years earlier in 2007 President Bush, unpopular at the time because of U.S. foreign policies going back to Central America's civil wars had visited. After his visit Mayan leaders held a ceremony to spiritually cleanse the sacred lands to restore peace and harmony to clean out the bad energy.

Just as my Halifax projects were coming to an end, I received a call from a former colleague that I had worked with at BC Hydro. He was now the Director of Procurement with MDA Systems Limited a Richmond BC based company in the aerospace and defense industry best known for the iconic Canada Arm and the Radarsat earth observation satellite systems.

MDA were having challenges resolving a contract dispute with the Federal Public Works over a project that wasn't going well. My friend asked if I would step in to negotiate a settlement and I said to him I know nothing about your industry and he said you don't need to know anything,

I know what you can do from working with you at BC Hydro and you're the guy that can negotiate a settlement to this problem.

This conversation led to a role at MDA Systems Dartmouth office as a Senior Contract Specialist with the primary role of negotiating a settlement to the contract dispute and also managing other contracts being carried out by the Dartmouth office.

The contract negotiation involved digging into the details, reviewing them against the contractual obligations and requirements; reporting strategy to senior management; and attending a number of negotiating sessions with Public Works and National Defense in Ottawa.

During the last round of negotiations, which had been back and forth over several months, a settlement was reached that protected MDA's interest and led to the successful conclusion of the contract. MDA's senior VP of finance was on the line for the final session and afterwards said to me. "They offered you a carrot on the end of a stick. You ate the carrot; grabbed the stick; and beat them into submission."

Following the success of this venture I went on to become part of the team that won the Electronics Warfare Systems Integrator contract for the Canadian Surface Combatant Program for the Canadian Navy and was also the contract specialists in charge of the TRITON project, the first major contract won by a Canadian defence contractor with NATO. This work was both interesting and challenging and it opened up a new field for me in information technology related to the surveillance and intelligence community.

The Director of Operations in Halifax had unexpectedly moved on and there was a void in leadership in that needed to be filled. I stepped up to the plate and offered my services on an interim basis until a replacement could be found and a short time later while performing in this role was asked by the COO of the company to accept the permanent position .

The parent company was going through a restructuring and the Canadian operations were up for sale and eventually purchased by a team of investors led by John Risley a proponent Nova Scotian industrialist who had made his fortune with Clearwater, turning the Atlantic lobster marketing and distribution company into a multi-billion-dollar enterprise.

On a companywide ZOOM call, MDA's President presented the

top-level organization chart for the major divisions of the company with offices in Richmond, Brampton, Montreal, and Halifax.

I was named as the Director of Operations for Halifax with the statement from the President that – "and of course, Michael will look after the Halifax office." Two weeks later I was on a conference call with the Senior Operations Director from Burnaby and a human resources specialist telling me that my services were no longer required; that my job was considered redundant; and that a three-month severance package is offered. I was able to negotiate an increase in my severance package from three to six months and was on the street again looking for work.

During the two-week period given to wind down my affairs, one of my senior management colleagues in the Halifax office out of the blue asked me if it was true that I had a role in taking down the Nova Scotia government some thirty years ago.

This was public knowledge so I couldn't deny it but the fact that he asked the question was suspicious to me. Why after a number of years working together would that point come up in conversation had it not been brought to his attention?

Then the penny dropped - Risley, MDA's new owner and chairman was close friends with Buchanan years earlier and no doubt when he saw my name on the organization chart gave instructions to get rid of me as he knew that I was not the kind of person that could be easily bought or manipulated.

My next job reconnected me with a major developer who I had come to know fifteen years earlier. His company was starting the Press Block project, based on a land lease deal with the Province of Nova Scotia and I was hired to provide my services to get the project underway.

This project brought me back to my old stomping grounds working across the street from Province House which I had been involved with restoring many years ago and where the Public Accounts Committee met, and Buchanan had his office.

This also brought me in contact with officials and the Department of Transportation and Infrastructure Renewal, the new name of the

Department of Government Services, where I was previously the Deputy Minister. On a staff level my involvement was appreciated and accepted by my former colleagues and the project came together as anticipated.

The timeline for this work was during the days of the COVID lockdowns, testing, and masking requirements. I knew when COVID was announced that this was a sham and chose not to go along with the unproven vaccine and other pointless mandates. Fortunately, I was able to set up a construction trailer on the job site where I could work alone and was not be required to deal with the company's COVID policies which I had spoken out against.

One afternoon while on site Premier Houstin was crossing Granville Street to enter his offices in One Government Place, and we made introductions while chatting over the project. Being a politically astute individual, it would not take Houston long to connect my past with the departure of his political mentor John Buchanan.

Near the completion of the site preparation work, the project was being staffed up by the developer's personnel from another project that was in the final stages of completion. Late one afternoon while driving home after work, the president called to tell me that my services were no longer required.

This did not surprise me as I sensed his frustration with me for not accepting without question some of his management decisions or perhaps, he was questioned by Houston or one of his minions wondering if my presence on the project was necessary. Maybe I was reading too much into the matter and his motivation was simply to save money.

Nevertheless, I was gone and a week later was providing consulting services to other prominent developers, project management and architectural firms in the region. As the saying goes, 'When one door closes, another door opens,' and that has certainly been my experience in life.

During my annual pacemaker checkup in 2018, the printout detected abnormal heart rhythms, the cardiologist arranged for an ultrasound and finding no issues recommended a follow up ultrasound in a year or so. In a routine checkup in January 2024 the irregular heart rates were again detected and although I was not experiencing any discomfort the previously recommended follow up ultrasound was booked for May 30th.

The technician took much longer this time to complete her scan and then asked if I could wait for a few minutes while she reviewed the results with the doctor. A few moments later she returned and asked me to wait a little longer as the results were being sent to cardiologist at the Halifax Infirmary. This time she returned with a cell phone in hand asking me to speak to the cardiologist who informed me that a tumor had been found inside of the left atrium of my heart and asked me to standby as someone would be contacting me to arrange for admission to the cardiac surgery floor.

Rather than wait at the clinic, I drove home, which was about ten minutes away, and called my wife Gail to tell her of the interesting discovery. Upon pulling into my driveway the cardiologist called back letting me know that the hospital admitting manager would be getting in touch. Later that morning a bed was confirmed and I told them to expect me to show up after supper.

The next day, Friday morning, the surgeon dropped by and told me I will be his first operation at 9:00 am on Monday morning. Later the surgical resident came by letting me know that the tumor referred to as a myxoma was about the size of a walnut and that the operation was urgent due to the risk of a piece of the tumor flaking off and causing an embolism or the tumor blocking a valve; in either case with dire consequences. I was also told that because of my excellent vitals and blood work results to expect all to go well.

Over the next couple of days, my focus was keeping my family upbeat and in good spirits, as I was not at all concerned with the outcome and as under all circumstances was taking it in stride.

Later on Monday morning as I was coming back to consciousness while the ICU nurse was removing my breathing tube he referred to me as the 'Rockstar of the ICU' and within a short time I was alert, receiving visitors and talking on the phone. That night the evening nurse asked if I could indicate my pain level from 1-10 and because she was asking for a number told her one, a couple of hours later when asking if there was any change, I told her to drop it down to zero.

While in post operation recovery there were issues with high heartrate and it did not matter if I was resting or walking. On one occasion, I had just woken up and was leaving the bathroom after brushing my teeth and standing by my bed speaking to my roommate when three nurses with a crash cart burst into the room asking if I was okay because my heart rate had shot up to 230 - I didn't feel a thing. The nurse's station monitor was showing that the rate stayed up in the range of 180 to 200 bpm all day and the duty nurse could not understand why I was not exhausted. Eventually the right medication was found to settle it down and when it was under control for 24 to 48 hours without further incident I was discharged. At discharge the resident surgeon commented again on my excellent health saying with a young healthy body like mine I should have no problems adjusting to the surgery.

My recovery regime included a lot of walking. In the first few days it was a challenge to walk to the end of the block and back, but in a couple of months my son Joe and I participated in the Dartmouth Natal Day race under the walking/jogging category. My daily 5 km walks continue and I can honestly say that I have never felt better and nor have I experienced the slightest bit of discomfort since the operation.

The lesson for me that has been reinforced by this experience is that health is largely affected by one's state of mind. If one chooses to maintain a positive state of consciousness and focuses on a healthy outcome, the body will respond accordingly. Afterall we are all individuated units of Divine Consciousness having a human experience, and acceptance and going with the flow in peace and equanimity in all circumstances pays off.

CHAPTER 21

Misinformation Age

E ver since my experiences in government I have been an avid consumer of and researcher on the story behind the story.

Being familiar with the origins of the mainstream media propaganda programs through Operation Mockingbird and my direct experience with media and government, I was aware that to the powers that be, the "truth" is what they say it is, not what it actually is and that it behooves the sincere seeker to investigate alternate sources of information; keep an open mind; and use their discernment in coming to a conclusion on any matter.

Through my search down the rabbit hole which have been going on for decades, there is for those who are willing to put in the time and effort, hundreds of books, thousands of articles and countless videos and documentaries on a wide variety of topics written or produced by leading thinkers and investigators that provide an alternative perspective to the public story line espoused by the controlled media.

The journey is likened to putting a complex jigsaw puzzle together with a lot of pieces missing or hidden that must be found to complete segments of the scene one piece at a time. Eventually when looked at from a higher perspective the diverse parts come together to form a coherent picture.

Much like in Plato's allegory "The Cave" we must step outside the confines of the illusion of reality to seek the truth and not settle for the shadows of truth that are projected in front of us.

Those in power including governments, bankers, and corporations collectively known as the "Deep State" control the people through saying one thing and doing the opposite. Once I understood this, all became much clearer – the Deep State will always act in their own best interests and use the ignorance of the public to their advantage. Our ignorance has been to our detriment as we march to our demise by handing over our individual power to institutional interest.

This influential elite is owned and controlled by the wealthiest families of the planet who exercise a powerful, profound, and clandestine control over the money supply and global politics. This control can be traced back to the time when these banking families discovered that it was more profitable to give loans to governments than to individuals.

Consequently, these families and their subservient beneficiaries have come to own the major banks and other businesses in this world, through which they have secretly and increasingly organized themselves as controllers of governments and arbiters of war and peace

Documents published by the United Nations with respect to Agenda 2021 and Agenda 2030, set out the game plan leading to one world government, central planning, and population control through catch phrases such as 'sustainable development' .

Henry Kissinger, a founding member of the elitist Trilateral Commission spawned today's drive toward the UN's 'Sustainable Development" outlined in the December 10, 1974, top-secret document entitled National Security Study Memorandum or NSSM-200, also known as The Kissinger Report through which he force-fed population control to the UN.

The primary purpose of population control/sustainable development efforts is to maintain access to the mineral resources of less-developed countries to support the western economy's insatiable requirement for increasing amounts of these minerals.

According to this plan, we must get by with less because there are now too many people on the planet consuming too many resources. They believe that our current lifestyles and consumptions patterns including high meat intake, convenience foods, use of motor vehicles and electric appliances in our suburban single-family homes are simply not sustainable.

The news pouring in daily to an overwhelming extent about how we're being scammed, poisoned, and domineered by politicians either doing the bidding of, or supported by multi-nationals, large corporations, non-elected think tanks, and other such global agencies.

Recent decades have seen a massive proliferation of such elite planning organizations, many operating openly with benign names like, the Rockefeller Foundation; the World Economic Forum; the Council on Foreign Relations, and the Institute for the Advancement of the Sciences to name but a few.

Thinking they are superior and knowing what's best for the world, they have funded and operated these think tanks, foundations, institutions, universities, and secret organizations in one form or another to formulate and hone their plans.

These global institutions - a network of corporate, government, media, and religious bodies - are withholding truth and information concerning everything from politics to physics while offering their own biased input, which is often completely bogus subterfuge designed to maintain control and create a public consensus.

Our governments are puppets of this Deep State and have become rotten to the core. Essentially, they are evil with a professed long-term agenda to systematically genocide we 'useless eaters '. We are the subjects of these internationalists who execute their experimental operations on a massive well-coordinated scale. Their aim to modify our minds and bodies as well as reduce our numbers is a repeatedly documented goal of these psychopaths.

We can no longer rely on politicians to fix the broken, irredeemable, and hopeless political system that they have created to serve themselves and their masters. As far as they are concerned the system is working just fine.

As a result of this brainwashing, a mindset of dependency of people on their so-called leaders has been firmly established. We have not only given over our control to our political leaders we also accept without question the authority of our religious, corporate, and state institutions to run our lives.

It is obvious that policies and programs adopted in recent years are designed to influence our lives to meet their goals through such initiates as the fifteen-minute smart cities, urbanization expansion through forced migration and open immigration policies, carbon taxes leading to higher living cost for food and shelter - all unsustainable for the masses - for the benefit of the few. Our shrinking middle class is paying the price while the underprivileged who are considered insignificant by the elite are being decimated.

The cunning techniques adopted to cull the population are through the control of healthcare to insure "healthy lives" through the promotion of universal health coverage which includes of course untested vaccines laced with poisons for all whether you need them or not.

On the one hand, we are offered universal access to "mental health" care while on the other state sponsored euthanasia programs which support death on demand. This will eventually lead to compulsory euthanasia for those with terminally illness whether mental or physical, followed by the aged - a path that Canada and other western nations are marching towards.

Then there is the promotion of "sexual and reproductive healthcare services" - code words for abortion and contraception leading to sterility in line with their eugenics goals. Historically, eugenicists have attempted to alter human gene pools by excluding people and groups judged to be inferior or promoting those judged to be superior – a form of scientific and medical racism with genetic selection criteria determined by whichever group has political power at the time.

The elites behind this agenda include unelected bankers, corporate leaders, philanthropist, and academia are making a concerted effort to control all segments of society through the influence of our politicians to adopt their policies at all levels of government

Our world leaders and policy makers have for centuries utilized Machiavellian principles and the most effective method used was the planning and implementation of a false flag event to achieve a goal. The name is derived from the military concept of flying false colors whereby a naval vessel flying the flag of another country would attack its own facilities or vessel in order to leave the public with the belief that retaliation is justified and necessary. People are inherently peace loving and don't want war. They must be manipulated into them by propaganda of political leaders and the policy makers above them who ultimately force the population to do their bidding by setting up an incident that leads to a reaction.

Those who see through the subterfuge are denounced as unpatriotic and sympathetic to the "enemy" and a threat to the security of the country. The motivation for all wars is the consolidation of power and control of resources to the ultimate benefit of the bankers and the military industrial complex who serve both sides and profit from each and every conflict.

False flags are not only used by our leaders to have us march into war, but they are also the easiest way to have the public accept draconian rules and mandates when they think their health and personal security is threatened.

All of the hype around pandemics share a common repetitive pattern. The assertions made as to the severity are always based on unfounded information, blatant medical or scientific errors from those pushing the agendas and contradictory information that is changed as the circumstances suit the shifting narrative.

The symptoms of the disease are often no more serious than a heavy dose of a seasonal flu or severe cold and although easily treated by time proven and effective remedies the official claim is that the false flag disease has only one condition and is linked to only one cause, in spite of evidence to the contrary.

In spite of the steps taken to control information, the truth of the false flags, with their constant repetitiveness, will serve as catalysts for a massive public wakeup calls. In time, through the declassification of public information, freedom of information requests, and undeniable testimony of whistleblowers, and independent researchers the truth will come to the surface.

Speaking truth to power only creates change if an educated populace says 'enough is enough.'

There is a clear and well-defined path from the non-elected policy makers at the very top of the control structure to we the people – the policy subjects at the very bottom.

The policy makers include the Bank of International Settlement (BIS) who ultimately control the money supply that influences global markets, trade, and national economics and the privately owned international network of central banks. Think tanks and other globalist groups work in conjunction with the bankers to formulate the policies and programs dictated from the top to be implemented across all nations of the world.

With resource allocations determined by the BIS and central banks they work in partnership to create worldwide monetary policy which effectively become the fiscal policy of nations that directly fund government spending allocated to these policies and programs.

Organizations such as the United Nations (UN), the International Monetary Fund (IMF), International Panel on Climate Change (IPCC), World Health Organization (WHO) and the World Bank adopt the policy directives from the policy makers and distribute them to those who are responsible to enforce the policies.

The Rothschild banking cartel has maintained tight-fisted control of the global money system through the BIS, IMF, the World Bank and the central banks of each nation, thus setting the value of all currency on earth. It is their control of the money supply which allows them to control world affairs from financing both sides of every conflict, through interlocking directorates in weapon manufacturing and energy production; along with the control of companies and governments executing global depopulation schemes, through genocide, the control of food supply, medicine, and all other basic human necessities.

The policy enforcers are the national governments including their civil service, crown corporations, police, military, courts, local state, and municipal governments and other statutory agencies who take their marching orders from the policy distributors. In otherwards, our governments at all levels are enforcing policies dictated from above – policies that the public have no say in. The fact is that our prime ministers and premiers are nothing more than figureheads for the central bankers and transnational corporations that really control this country and ultimately call the shots.

These policy enforcers also include medical authorities supported by alliances involving both regulators and industry as equal partners. Scientific and technical discussions are held to arrive at the testing procedures which are required to ensure and assess the safety, quality, and efficacy of medicines. Such groups falsify information and manipulate data to fabricate the results that they want you to believe.

Canada Border Services Agency (CBSA) is a policy enforcer mandated to provide integrated border services that support national security and public safety priorities and facilitate the free flow of persons and goods. They were used by our government to enforce travel restrictions by shutting down our borders based on the false science that claimed that those with a seasonal cold and flu constituted a national emergency to our public health. This is an example of a policy directive from the WHO an unelected privately funded agency in the business of making money on ineffective and untested vaccines that eventually killed millions.

In fact, we know now that in Nova Scotia, the health department has no records of the genetic sequencing of the COVID virus isolated from tissue from any person in Nova Scotia diagnosed with COVID-19. They relied on false science dictated from above to enforce mandatory vaccinations, lockdowns, and masking mandates in lock step with every other province and territory in Canada and for that matter around the world.

Policy enforcers collaborate with the selected health, medical, environmental, and other such pseudo authorities to justify the policies they are directed to enforce from COVID mandates to carbon taxes to diversity and inclusion. The enforcers are supported by policy spin doctors including the mainstream media, government communication agencies, public relations authorities, fact checkers, social media platforms all with specialist skills to combat "misinformation". In the information environment, whether we refer to misinformation, fake news, or information warfare, the purpose is all the same – to formulate and spread propaganda.

The propagandists include anti hate campaigners set up to stop the spread of online hate and disinformation through research, public campaigns, and policy advocacy. These mouth pieces along with their government sponsors lobby social media platforms to stop providing services to individuals who they claim are promoting "hate and misinformation", including populist movement, anti-vaccine advocates, and climate deniers. They are the storm troopers that campaign to restrict and discredit any organization or personality that sees through the deceitfulness.

Policy propagandists have an information warfare network in place to control and protect access to the "official" information for public dissemination. They use technology and innovation as a kind of superhighway for the dissemination of their message. This information warfare network acquires and uses fabricated information brought forward by countless numbers of dedicated researchers engaged to destroy opposing information systems and disrupt the truthful and accurate flow of facts.

Information warfare touches so many aspects of our society. The policy propogandist have formed a community of interest, bringing together practitioners, policy makers, and thinkers from within government departments, academia, industry, and the international community to achieve their goals. Using psychological manipulation, disinformation, misinformation, censorship, and propaganda, their mission is to collaborate and exploit cyber information to convince the public to accept and believe in their policies. Big data, autonomy, machine learning, social sciences, social media, and global connectivity all play an increasingly important role in our lives and all are tools at their disposal being used against us.

We the people are the subjects of these policies that cascade down through the system to exploit, indoctrinate, and enslave us. And to add insult to injury, we pay through taxation and public borrowing to establish their plans for complete global control. The public must have the right to participate in and make policy decisions that impact their livelihood...a right that will never be given under the current governance model. The character and attributes of any community that make it unique are at risk if top-down rules and regulations are inadvertently adopted because they were not clearly understood or challenged. Despite pressures from our elected representatives, we must advocate for a bottom-up approach for the benefit of all to chart our own vision for the future.

Bottom-up public participation will foster a stronger accountability process and balance of power among communities, individual citizens, and service providers. It will improve the quality and sustainability of the program or policy stimulating development and grow in positive ways. Through the process communities as a whole and its citizens as individuals and groups will strengthen bonds that hold them together.

This is why each and every individual interested in freedom from tyranny must strive to build a network of those working in diverse fields to counter these disruptive mind controlling propaganda techniques. This mind control project has become so successful that people will do things that are contrary to common sense.

Through the failure to go within and use our intuitive discernment skills, we have allowed the institutions of government to take over our thinking. All the while being caught up in the proverbial rate race that harnesses our time, labor, and energy for the enrichment of the powerful elite.

To free ourselves, we must individually and collectively wake up and take responsibility for our own individual truth by speaking up against this government adopted disinformation program. We can know and understand the forces of light to mean the promoting, the dispensing, and the sharing of truthful information - while on the other hand the forces of darkness perpetuate lies while controlling and withholding the truth.

The Deep State controlled media's number one objective is to keep the truth hidden. Once we acknowledge that, we come to the realization that everything we are fed is propaganda. This will put us on a path to mental and spiritual freedom, but it takes some doing, and takes guts to openly see past the false information we're being fed.

Instead of expanding our access to information; instead of inspiring individuals to dig for truth and research for reality, the institutional media and their controllers are constricting the field of information. This is particularly obvious with recent challenges to the concept of an open, equal internet for everyone, regardless of device, application or platform used and content consumed. Net neutrality is overwhelmingly supported by the majority of the population, while institutions are seeking to destroy it.

This tightening of ideas has reached the point that anything which presents a challenging to the mainstream narrative is being disparaged, or outright censored, while at the same time, pugnacious propaganda is put forth through the global media who refuse to genuinely analyze or criticize the actions of their government sponsors.

A clear example is the distinct absence of any pacifists in the mainstream news media even questioning our government's policy of aggressive global intervention. Our governments consistently incite conflict with other nations under the guise of defending our democracy through spending billions on military and humanitarian aid while trying to convince us that this will lead to 'peace'. Moreover, the media repeatedly obscures and falsifies information, while blacking out important stories completely. The actions of the media demonstrate that it is working to advance corporate and government agendas - birds of a feather flock together.

The information age could completely shift the current power structures of the world in favor of individuals instead of institutions. Just look at the countless global events being reported by individuals through the underground news and compare it to the selective, politically biased fear-offerings of the institutional mainstream media. As a result, public confidence in mainstream news has steadily declined over recent years while "alternative media" has risen in its place, filling the void of real news, views and analysis that go unheard and unexamined in institutional and corporate circles.

The information age not only invites but requires that we expand our consciousness and our comprehension, not limit it. We do not need to funnel the pool of information into the narrow mainstream, we need to expand our minds and increase the numbers of sources of information. We don't need corrupted governments or media corporations controlled by the wealthy elite telling us what is true or what is important. The more information we have access to the more easily we can use our discernment to spot biased untruthful information and act accordingly

Media complicity is clear and their influence is waning rapidly as grass roots community actions and citizen journalists proliferate. The fact that a realistic, awake, and aware perspective of seeing and reporting on an alternative point of view and exposing fake news for what it is has been portrayed as "conspiratorial" says it all. Naturally they have to decry anything that opposes them. In reality, the fake news pushed by the Deep State media is the real conspiracy, and it is they who are clearly executing a stated agenda, one we are now fully awakening to.

CHAPTER 22

Canada Our Home
and Native Land

C anada is a posterchild country for the planned takeover and control by this special interest group of International Bankers that exist to subjugate the entire world under a one world dictatorship known as the One World Government or the New World Order.

This group is not a fan of democracy and has initiated a silent global coup d'état to capture governments by penetrating cabinets, political parties, bureaucracies, municipal leaders, industry, and institutions through their World Economic Forum (WEF) Young Global Leaders program. Not only has Prime Minister Trudeau and half of his cabinet been indoctrinated and sold out to the WEF's agenda, so have key players in opposition party along with those of our legislatures and municipal governments as well. In this way, governments are used as a tool of the Deep State to rule the entire world by this unelected dictatorship under the pretext of the public private partnerships that the globalists control.

As far as the formation of the Dominion of Canada is concerned, our history provides clear evidence that the people did not want this union of the provinces of Upper and Lower Canada, New Brunswick, and Nova Scotia - particularly not Nova Scotians, who having the most to lose, voted not to join. Nevertheless, despite strong opposition Britain forged on and enacted the British North America Act (BNA) later referred to as the Constitution Act, and took control of our land, laws and resources under a Governor General of Canada who reported to and operated on behalf of the Queen with whom executive government and authority of and over Canada continued to be vested. The Governor General became the de facto Chief Executive Officer or Administrator, and the Commander -in-Chief of Canada on behalf of and in the name of the Queen – for all intents a purpose a dictator.

The Statute Law Revision Act of 1893 repealed Section 2 of the BNA Act; this provision of the Act referred to Her Majesty the Queen and extended also to the Heirs and Successors of Her Majesty, Kings and Queens of the United Kingdom of Great Britain and Ireland. As a result of repealing reference to present and future monarchy, adjudication of and authority over the Constitution Act shifted from the Queen and her Heirs to the Chancery Court in the United Kingdom.

Nevertheless, by the command of His Majesty King George V, an heir and successor to Queen Victoria, despite him having been removed from the British North America Act, a commission was signed in 1935 appointing the Right Honorable Lord Tweedsmuir to be Governor General and Commander-in-Chief of our Dominion of Canada with a continuance of all the powers and privileges of that office. This appointment was fraudulent and unlawful and it violated the Constitution Act as amended.

Through the Constitution Act the British Parliament allocated certain powers to the two levels of government referred to as the legislatures or provinces and the parliament or the federal government. The parliament and each provincial legislature are sovereign bodies within its sphere of influence, possessed of exclusive jurisdiction to legislate with regard to the subject matters assigned to it under the Act and neither is permitted to delegate to or receive from the other the powers with which it has been endowed.

The provinces have the power of direct taxation in order to raise revenue for provincial purposes. This power cannot legally be transferred to the federal government. Consequently, income tax, even provincial income tax in all provinces except Quebec is illegal because of the tax collection agreements between the provinces and the federal government enshrined in the Constitution Act.

The parliament of Canada does however have the power to raise revenue by any other means except by direct taxation, and since direct taxation is the exclusive jurisdiction of the provinces, the federal government has no business poking its fingers in that pie.

The provisions of the Constitution Act did not stop the parliament from fraudulently passing the Federal Income Tax Act introduced in 1917 with the explicit purpose, being to pay the cost of the First World War, a debt which was paid off in 1929 yet the tax remains to this day. In 1918, the Canadian government formally introduced Daylight Saving Time as a way to increase production during wartime. Daylight savings time is what was called 'war time' - we're still on war time and the income tax is a war tax.

The real reason for the introduction of Federal Income Tax Act was in order to service the national debt that was growing at a massive and unprecedented rate due to the introduction to the Bank Act of 1913 which turned over the control of banking to the private bankers. The federal government gave its money creation powers to the private charter banks in 1913 and from that time forward borrowed itself into debt. Because indirect taxation was the exclusive domain of the provinces, the federal parliament borrowed from the banks to raise revenue. The result was the establishment of an energetic and dynamic banking sector that grew quickly and without regulation; serving the economic needs of an emerging national economy and helping fuel an economic boom .

There was another option - rather than raise money through borrowing from international bankers or through federal income tax; with prudent management of royalty revenues from the estimated $33.2 trillion worth of natural resources, Canada could have more than covered the cost of the services that it is obligated to provide under the constitution. The federal and provincial governments have not come to an equitable agreement on the sale and management of our natural resources. Consequently, the public suffers economically under burgeoning national debt loads while the global corporations that exploit our resources on behalf of the international bankers become ridiculously wealthy - the bankers own and control it all.

If the government rather than the banks was issuing our money as they are required to do by the Constitution Act, then we would have no taxation whatsoever at the federal level other than taxation of corporations on the extraction and use of our national resources. This wealth would then be turned over to us minus that portion which the government used to provide the services that we authorize under the constitution.

It is self-evident that the government owes us and should be paying us annually. Instead, we labor to the point of exhaustion in order to create wealth for the international bankers to control our governments, our resources, our institutions, and our lives. If we the citizens had the control of our country and the government acted as our trustee with respect to the control and management of our natural resources then our economic future would change dramatically.

This power given to the private banks to create money and control credit was an unlawful action by politicians and bureaucrats and outside the powers of parliament as stipulated in the Constitution Act. In essence, our government handed the control of our wealth to the money changers, the international bankers.

Beyond Income Tax, the purpose of taxation of any kind, even the courts and license fees, speeding tickets, parking tickets and the like, is all designed to take the bank's unlawful fiat currency out of circulation and return it to the banks. It is inconceivable that the private banks actually create all of our money out of nothing, loan it to us at interest and we are required to pay this money and the interest back to the banks who produced it out of thin air.

However, this is the system we operate under. World banking uses 'Babylonian Black-Magic', the secret art of making money from nothing and using the power of pernicious usury to accumulate interest. The Rothschild family perfected the art and set up a private global fiat banking system that specializes in making counterfeit money from nothing - adopting ruinous moneylending practices for using what should have been our own money in the first place.

Once we cut through the smoke and mirrors and get past the idea that government needs money to provide us with roads and healthcare and pay interest on the national debt, we come to the realization that taxes are simply a means of stealing our wealth and enslaving us all. Income taxes, all other taxes, the court fines, license fees, speeding tickets, offence fines of every sort in the country are for the benefit of the banks. It is simply to extract money from our society and return it to its creator, the banks.

Those who realize what is happening and ask the court for the name of the true creditor or recipients of the fines imposed by the 'legal system' are always refused this information by the judge. The true creditors in such cases, and the ultimate recipient of the fines, are the bankers to which the bankrupt governments are indebted to. The entire structure of what currently passes for government is actually a conglomerate of private corporations that are owned by World Bankers and run by aristocratic politicians and civil servants.

One simply has to look at the proliferation of Public Private Partnerships (PPPs) that have sprung up in recent decades involved with all aspects of major infrastructure development from financing, management, maintenance and operations of large-scale health care, education, transportation, and municipal projects. These PPPs typically include high upfront costs paid for by the taxpayer, limitations placed on meaningful community consultations, and a procurement process that is neither competitive or transparent. If there is a PPP project in your province, know that you are being taken to the cleaners, and there is nothing you can do about it.

The true nature of government in Canada is not that of a democracy, but rather a combination of governmental and private corporate interests – known otherwise as fascism. We no longer have government of the people, by the people and for the people but instead have government of the people, by the politicians, for the bankers. We the people of Canada must come together in an effort to bring about the changes necessary to save our government and sever the chains of bondage that bind us to the international bankers. The present fiat currency system is being used to create money out of nothing by the private banks for the sole purpose of stealing our wealth.

We are the collateral for the national debt. Our birth certificates are bought and sold and our future earning potential is used as collateral for the worthless pieces of paper currency that has enslaved us all. Our names, as written on our original birth certificate with each name beginning with a capital letter followed by lowercase letters, legally represents our physical body as an individual man or a woman - a living human being.

As a living being it is unlawful to contract with corporations. Living beings' contract with living beings and corporations with corporations. To get around this technicality, the government has created a mirror image of us and as such they have taken control of us because we admit to being a legal fiction or strawman by using the all-capital name that is shown on the certified copy of our birth certificates at the time of registration. This name in all caps certificate is our maritime admiralty product code with a unique serial number attached to it.

When issuing contracts for government or corporate services of any kind, the government or corporation as the case may be show our names with each letter being capitalized such as on your driver's license or any credit card bill. By creating this legal fiction, we are being incorporated as a PERSON, and this obligates us to play by the rules of Contract Law and the Bills of Exchange Act as adjudicated by judges appointed and paid for by the government through the courts under their control.

When Canadian courts operate under admiralty or maritime jurisdiction, it means that when we enter the court, we are in a court martial type of proceeding where we have no rights and we are not protected by the constitution. Admiralty law courts conduct their trials without a jury, and the law is what the judge says it is. The gold-fringed flag is the War flag which denotes Admiralty or "guilt-presumed" martial law. When we see a gold-fringed flag in a court it sends the signal that we are under Admiralty Law denoting international rule, where everything is based upon "the law of the High Seas," where the admiral/judge has complete discretion. Judges will refuse to replace the flag with one without a fringe when asked by defendants who know the score because that changes the law under which the court is sitting

The gold-fringed flag trumps the Constitution which is merely a discretionary document. That means, if that flag is present, the Constitution is suspended and the constitutional rights we think we have are non-existent. Not only our courts, but our federal parliament, senate and several provincial legislatures fly the admiralty flag – another indication that our elected represented are not the servants of the people. The "House of Commons" in Ottawa has nothing in common with the public.

Admiralty courts are nothing more than courts of military rule conducted by a judge under the rules of summary procedures. Juries do not apply, thereby eliminating the power of jury nullification, where a jury returns a Not Guilty verdict even though jurors believe beyond reasonable doubt that the defendant has broken the law.

In the City of London, the Templars established their headquarters at a church/temple called Temple Bar which was also known as the Crown Temple. It is the Crown Temple that controls the financial, legal and court system of Canada and many other countries. Our governments are all subsidiaries of and the ruling Monarch in England is subordinate to this Crown.

All bar associations are directly linked to the International Bar Association and the Inns of Court at Crown Temple. Anytime you hear somebody refer to the Bar Association, they are talking about a British system that has nothing to do with a country's sovereignty or the constitutional rights of its people.

The courts are presided over by judges appointed and paid for by the government along with the rest of the judicial system including crown attorney and court staff. Pursuing the truth and expecting your rights to be fairly adjudicated by a biased justice system does not matter. The purpose of the court is to convict you and the only thing that matters to the court is bringing in revenue to pay their salaries.

It does not matter what the truth is, it is evident that judges are biased. Bringing obvious bias to the court's attention has no effect. The courts will continue to rule in favor of public policies based on the government's agenda, at the expense of justice and truth. Know that the government's agenda is synonymous with and endorsed by the Deep State. If a judge acts in an unbiased manner frequently rendering truly unbiased decisions, then their future on the bench will be in jeopardy from those very individuals who appointed them in the first place. Our seasoned politicians know that this is how things are and so do senior government administrators, judges, lawyers, and insider 'journalists'.

The courts are stacked against us and we can expect to lose if we take on any issues related to the unlawfulness of the constitution, the lack of constitutional support for the Income Tax Act of Canada, the lack of constitutional support for provincial income taxes being transferred to the federal government, and the issue concerning the banks controlling our money and issuing fiat currency out of nothing.

Over and above all else in the Canadian Constitution, the fact remains that it was a British statute and that it would be interpreted ultimately by a British-based and British-oriented court, which would likely bring to bear upon it all the standards and techniques of the British judicial tradition. The Government of Canada aside from being a criminal organization having no lawful authority to exist is nothing more than a puppet government operating under the auspices of these international banking families.

For all intents and purposes, the Canadians public are paying a war tax, under war time, under an emergency war powers act, and the courts are war courts. Could it be that the Government of Canada is at war with Canadians? That is the only rational conclusion that a reasoned evaluation of the facts can come to.

Every law that is passed in this country is ordered by the Privy Council who in turn takes orders from this international banking oligarchy. This simply means that we are being governed by a foreign hidden an unelected governmental dictatorship and this will remain so until authorized by the people of Canada through the writing and acceptance of a valid constitution.

Black's Law Dictionary defines constitution as follows, "The organic and fundamental law of a nation or state which may be written or unwritten establishing the character and conception of its government, laying the basic principles to which its internal life is to be conformed, organizing the government, and regulating, distributing, and limiting the functions of its different departments, and prescribing the extent and manner of the exercise of sovereign powers. A character of government deriving its whole authority from the governed, the written instrument agreed upon by the people of the union."

Under this definition, Canada has no constitution because the constitution as a document establishing and limiting the powers of government written and ratified by the people of the nation does not exist and has never existed in Canada's history. Not only do we not have a constitution, the BNA Act of the Imperial Parliament of England that Trudeau so deceitfully repatriated and called a constitution is being routinely violated by the federal government. The federal government has intruded upon provincial government powers in areas of taxation, property, and civil rights with the gun law, health care, the national energy program and the list goes on.

A true Constitution does not belong either to the parliament or to the legislatures, it belongs to the citizens of the country. It is a written instrument agreed upon by the people defining the rules under which the various departments and officers of the government shall operate and it establishes the protection of the rights to which the citizens are entitled. Most importantly, the constitution cannot be changed without the authority of people who established it.

It is a well-known to those who are willing to dig deep and look at the evidence that taking on the international banking cartel and exposing their modus operandi can have dire consequences.

On July 2nd, 1881 James Garfield a former President of the United States said this about the money system, "Whosoever controls the volume of money in any country is absolute master of all industry and commerce and when you realize that, the entire system is very easily controlled one way or another buy a few powerful men of the top, you will not have to be told how periods of inflation and depression originate." On September 19th, 1881, within a few weeks of making that statement, President Garfield was assassinated.

Another courageous US President John F Kennedy took on the international bankers with his attempt to reform the money system for the benefit of the American people. Kennedy reasoned that by returning to the constitution, which states that only Congress shall coin and regulate money, the soaring national debt could be reduced by not paying interest to the bankers of the Federal Reserve System, who print paper money then loan it to the government at interest.

According to the Constitution of the United States, only Congress has the authority to control and regulate the value of money However, since 1913 the constitution has been ignored by creation and existence of the Federal Reserve Act, which has given a private owned corporation the power and authority to "create" and coin the money of United States.

The Federal Reserve is comprised of twelve private credit monopolies who have been given the authority to control the supply of the "Federal Reserve Notes," interest rates and all the other monetary and banking dealings. The way the Federal Reserve works is this: the private credit monopolies "create", (print), Federal Reserve Notes that are then "lent" to the American government. This is a circular affair in that the government grants the FED power to create the money, which the FED then loans back to the government, charging interests.

The government levies income taxes to pay the interest on the debt. The Federal Reserve Act and the sixteenth amendment which gave congress the power to collect income taxes, were both passed in 1913. The Federal Reserve Notes are not backed by anything of "intrinsic" value. (i.e., gold or silver).

On June 4, 1963, Kennedy signed a Presidential decree, Executive Order 11110, which stripped the Federal Reserve Banking System of its power to loan money to the United States Federal Government at interest. By giving the U.S. Treasury the Constitutional authority to coin U.S. money once again, EO 11110 would thus prevent the national debt from rising due to "usury" that the American people are charged for "borrowing" these notes.

Kennedy knew that, if Congress coined and regulated money, as the Constitution states, the national debt would be reduced by not paying interest to the international banking monopolies. This in itself would have allowed the American people the freedom to use all the money they have earned, enabling the economy to grow. Although Executive Order 11110 is still in effect, there has been no U.S. President with the courage to follow through with it.

In a speech made to Columbia University on Nov. 12, 1963, ten days before his assassination, President John Fitzgerald Kennedy said: "The high office of the President has been used to foment a plot to destroy the American's freedom and before I leave office, I must inform the citizen of this plight." Kennedy was trying to rein in the power of the Federal Reserve. It is highly likely that the forces opposed to such action might have played at least some part in the assassination.

The Canada financial situation is no different than that of American. We have to realize the awesome power and wealth of these international bankers and how they control us through fear and intimidation and we must come together to do something about it. We individually can do nothing but collectively we have all of the power.- the power of truth.

In summary, Canadians have been without lawful federal and provincial governments since 1931 when a fraudulent monarchy was imposed upon us. While the Crown of the City of London secretively assumed control as a colonial ruler putting us into deeper oppression as a subservient protectorate saddling us with massive debt based on counterfeit money borrowed from foreign bankers.

Canada has no legitimately recognized constitution for our provincial or our federal governments. The alleged constitution ratified by the Constitutions Act of 1982 was not consented to by the people, making it an unequivocal sham. This fact and the insertion of the notwithstanding clause totally disaffirms it as the ultimate law of Canada. In addition, admiralty law imposed upon us by this massive fraud through unlawful and ultra vires legislation and unlawful judicial process further negates the constitution. Judges use legal fraud and deception to entrap Canadians and to use their foreign maritime admiralty jurisdiction where individual rights are not recognized.

If you still believe that the government is there to support you and look after your best interests and that if you keep your hands clean, obey the law, and pay your taxes, all will be fine – you are sadly mistaken.

CHAPTER 23

The Party's Over

Most conflicts in society are cultivated by our leaders because control is easier if we are divided on the issues. When people are fighting amongst themselves then they cannot organize to take charge of their lives. Tyranny thrives in this culture of dividing and conquering the enemy. In a system where a few elitists scheme to keep all wealth and control for themselves, we the people exploited become their enemies.

To control the many by the few is vital to form political parties. Party politics produced the ideal structure through which party members of all levels of government can be controlled by the Deep State. Instead of having to force their will upon hundreds of legislators and party followers, all that has to be done is to force their agenda upon those who control the party system who in turn will enforce it upon their members.

Simply said, if someone wants to progress in politics, they first need to join a party and then keep the ruling elite satisfied by doing and saying what they are told. And to make sure that politicians do as they are told, detailed information is kept on all politicians including senior bureaucrats who form the government whether in power or in opposition. These secrets can be revealed at any time to assure that those contemplating such ethical behavior as speaking their mind rather than supporting the party's talking points are brought into line through fear of secrets becoming public. In fact, those that hold key positions of power and influence are the ones with the most damming secrets to hide for anything from financial fraud to trafficking that keeps them in line for fear of public exposure.

It's the same with doctors, lawyers, scientists, clergy, and other highly regulated hierarchical professions; keep your head down, don't rock the boat, and certainly don't oppose anything significant through personal conscience against the wishes of the establishment. Real personal 'progress' in any of these regulated professions demands that you play the role and follow the script given to you.

The Deep State with their tentacles in the election process from start to finish including choosing the date of the election, the selection of party candidates, the vote counting methodologies and any judicial review process can pretty well fabricate any outcome that will serve their long-term objective.

In the 2021 Nova Scotia provincial election close to 50% of eligible voters did not cast a ballot and in the 2024 election it was worse with only 45% participation. That is almost four-hundred and fifty thousand voters; people who lost faith in the democratic system because it no longer represents them. This dismal voting turnout is a clear indication that elections today are irrelevant because the public knows that elections are rigged.

In fact, it doesn't matter who you vote for, the Deep State who control all political parties decide which government gets installed. The puppet masters make sure that the political party that will best serve their interest have their turn at the trough and when it is time for change in response to public frustration and anger an opposition party is given their chance to belly up.

In parliaments and legislative assemblies around the world we have individuals known as "Whips" A whip is an official of a political party whose task is to ensure party discipline. This means ensuring that members of the party vote according to the party platform rather than according to their own individual ideology or the will of their constituents.

Whips are the party's enforcers. They work to ensure that their fellow legislators attend voting sessions and vote according to their party's official policy. Members who vote against party policy risk being expelled from the party. The fact that whips exist and operate openly is proof of corruption within politics and the general disdain that politicians have for the will of the people.

Any dissension or disagreements within the party system has been used as a club to remove those speaking up on behalf of their constituents who elected them. Provincially two popular women were both removed for actively opposing the party leader - issues key to their constituents fell on deaf ears. It is obviously apparent that simply questioning party leadership and standing up for the truth continues to have dire consequences.

For example, in Nova Scotia Alana Paon a member of the Conservative Party under Premier Tim Houston was ejected from the caucus allegedly over the accessibility of her constituency office and other trumped-up excuses but more than likely because she introduced a provocative private member's bill "An Act to Eliminate Political Party Whips". An earlier example of political retribution for not doing as you are told was the expulsion of Elizabeth Smith-McCrossin, the MLA for Cumberland North who was removed from the Progressive Conservative Caucus by the then PC Leader Tim Houston.

Smith-McCrossin had received a warning from the Liberal government in power not to support her constituents who gathered at the NS/NB border to protest COVID restrictions. Rather than support Smith-McCrossin and her constituents, Houstin caved to the 'powers that be' who were setting the COVID policies for all political parties to follow and ejected her from the party.

In spite of being told she would not be allowed to run for the PC Party in future elections, Smith-McCrossin went on to run successfully as an Independent in both 2021 and 2024 and continues to effectively represent the aspirations and needs her constituents with more influence in the Legislature than if she were a party backbencher.

People are fed up, and there is a growing realization that something must be done about it. We must help ourselves become sovereign and free by creating alternatives to move positive change by governing ourselves and taking responsibility for our lives out from under the control of corrupt governments entirely. We have arrived here because of the accumulated evidence overwhelmingly proves that the status quo is a fraud.

We have to free ourselves from this corrupt system that benefits the few at the expense of the many and take control of our own destiny. Deep down we know that freedom must not only benefit the individual it must advance the aspirations and needs of the collective. With freedom comes responsibility and to truly have freedom we must have the maturity to accept the consequences of our actions. We can no longer blame our governments, our religions, our parents, our teachers, and our societies for the choices we make.

Blaming others limits our own freedom by not being aware and responsible for and owning our thoughts, feelings, decisions, and behavior. We must lead by example, sharing our message of empowerment, worthiness, connection, and love with the world, through our own unique authentic voices of truth. We cannot sit back and allow someone else to take the action necessary to protect us; we must do it ourselves.

Otherwise, we will be like the German citizens Martin Niemöller who wrote after the Second World War:

*"First, they came for the socialists, and I did not
speak out—because I was not a socialist.
Then they came for the trade unionists, and I did not speak
out—because I was not a trade unionist. Then they came for the
Jews, and I did not speak out—because I was not a Jew.
Then they came for me—and there was no one left to speak for me."*.

These powerful words about guilt and responsibility still resonate today, serving as a denunciation of passivity and indifference. Courageous individuals willing to stand apart from the crowd and become self-masters will lead the way to transcend the status quo and forge a new future.

As a towering lighthouse shines brightly through thick dark fog, guiding the way home to those who are lost at sea, we must stand tall and share the unique frequency of our own powerful force of enlightened truth to help others find the way. By each of us doing this, collectively we will reach a critical mass, a tipping point of awakening whereby a new paradigm is created. Through rejecting the authority of institutions, we will embrace our individual sovereign authority to which we as spiritual beings have been endowed.

We will either have a society based on competition for control or a society based on cooperation for independence. These two competing systems are mutually exclusive. The materialistic model is based on competition and conquest with a goal of total central control; while the holistic model is based on cooperation and seeking harmony with the goal of individual liberty and preservation of human rights. These opposing ideas are not compatible and only one will prevail.

When we come to realize that we are one with our fellow human beings, we become capable of making the transition. It is a transformation that begins within the individual and as it grows, collectively we will reform the way in which society is organized. When this happens, governments will fall and our entire social structure will change. It will be both challenging and rewarding at the same time as everyone on earth will come to own their sovereignty and freedom.

An independent leaderless society would allow all people to lead their own advancement instead of leaving this role to others. It would allow the average person to become empowered and capable of wonderful feats of personal achievement while simultaneously enabling others by their example.

CHAPTER 24

The Independent Initiative

I n early August of 2023, I watched an interview conducted by Dr. Reiner Fuellmich with Peter Mac Issac, a former provincial game warden speaking on the corrupt and inept management practices particularly related to the devastating forest fires in Nova Scotia and across Canada. Fuellmich is the courageous American German lawyer spearheading a second Nuremberg tribunal with the support of thousands of lawyers and medical professionals worldwide with a class action lawsuit to prosecute those responsible for the COVID-19 scandal. For his outspoken efforts on behalf of humanity, the German court system is utilizing the political practice of "lawfare" with fabricated charges designed to smear and silence him. He is currently incarcerated in a maximum-security prison during the prolonged and unjust trial.

In the interview Mac Isaac proposed that the corrupt party controlled political system is broken and not worth saving and advocated for an independent grass roots movement as an alternative. The content and delivery of Peter's message was spoken with integrity and he came across as authentic and honest. This was music to my ears, finally I realized that I was not alone and that there were others in the province that shared my conviction that change was necessary so I reached out immediately to set up a meeting.

The next morning, we got together for coffee and it was as if we had known each other all of our lives. Peter shared with me that as well as being a provincial game warden, he was a forest fire fighter, a wildlife specialist and has produced three seasons of a popular international fishing and hunting television series. He had run unsuccessfully for the NS Progressive Conservative Party in 2012 and served as a past president of the federal Conservative Party Halifax West thus gaining firsthand insight into the broken political system. We shared our deep concern over the corruption and incompetence in the failed party system and the planned destruction of our country, and he asked if I would come back the next day to meet his friend Paul Westhaver, a colleague with similar convictions. Paul and Peter were working on a concept to start a movement to run independent candidates in the next Provincial election.

Paul's involvement with the movement came as a result of earlier investigations into the temperament of the people of Nova Scotia regarding the state of party-oriented governance. A solution oriented Professional Engineer with a broad career exposure, he is dedicated to process analysis, improvement, and renewal. He has and continues to be an advocate for those unjustly treated by our corrupt judicial system and has effectively used the power of freedom of information requests to obtain damning evidence to support his advocacy work.

We share a common view that the current state of affairs of the Nova Scotia governance model is antiquated and fundamentally corrupt to the point where popular apathy is essential to maintaining the rigid, top-down party system - a political system where the parties are for all practical purpose indistinct from each other. The election of independent candidates has the potential to dramatically change our broken political landscape. Power will no longer be in the hands of broken parties run by tyrants who are controlled by backroom unelected individuals we don't know and never see. Independents responsible only to those who elect them is the only way to give control back to the people where it belongs.

We agreed to work together to make it happen and within days we were in touch with Salvatore Vetro the founder of a similar movement in British Columbia who with his colleague Rick Dignard formed a non-profit called the Independent BC Initiative. Aligning on common goals we could see the benefit of such initiatives being established in every province in Canada. With the support of our newfound compatriots, within two weeks we had incorporated our own non-profit society the "Independent NS Initiate" modelled on the work done in BC.

The party system restricts the entry of quality candidates due to rigorous vetting processes that eliminate those that question party doctrine. We believe that the best representatives are those who truly understand their constituents' concerns, without being beholden to party interests. Independent candidates can prioritize the collective need above all else and are not bound by ineffective and self-serving rigid party policies.

The system cannot be changed without a drastic makeover. At some point we allowed this system of control over our lives, consequently we have the power to dissolve it and replace it with an entirely new system.

Through social networking the Independent NS Initiative Society has grown to comprise a group of concerned citizens committed to educating voters about the electoral process, with a focus on running independent candidates for election as Members of the Legislative Assembly (MLA) across NS, in future election.

We are not a political party, nor are we associated with any political party. We exist simply to educate voters about "A NEW WAY TO VOTE"; to help communities recruit an Independent Candidate to represent them with honesty and integrity; to offer guidance to communities on running town hall meetings; and to prepare Independent Candidates with information about their MLA career.

Our information strategy revolves around two key pillars, social media, and debates. We recognize the power of digital platforms to connect directly with the people of Nova Scotia. By focusing on the "Town Hall" concept of social media, we encourage engagement with the public in real-time dialogue, openly sharing alternative perspectives, and listening to public feedback. Community engagement to arrive at clear, concise, and understandable policy documents will guide the growth and meet the aspirations of our communities into the future.

We want to showcase our dedication, expertise, and passion for the critical issues that matter most to our community and our province. Through transparent and insightful discussions, we're confident that a shared vision for a better Nova Scotia will resonate with voters.

It is time for the people's voices to be heard. This movement will set the stage for a new era of representation and participation by independent and free men and women of our Province, focusing primarily on three crucial issues that currently directly impact the people of Nova Scotia.

Protection of our Children

Our governments have launched a multi-front war on children through our social welfare, judicial, health, and education system in an effort to reduce the population and destroy traditional family values.

We are committed to safeguarding our children from agendas which advocate among other things premature sexualization and gender confusion through pop-culture pervasion; pseudo health and vitality through forced vaccinations, GMO food, and fluoridated water; and the trafficking of our children for nefarious purposes. This issue is close to our hearts as it is the foundation upon which strong healthy families must be rebuilt and maintained.

Independents will not be bound by party policies dictated by non-elected donors and lobbyists. Independent candidates will be able to advocate for age-appropriate education; true peer reviewed science in the efficacy of additives to our food and water; and full disclosure of government information in order to protect our children's innocence and well-being.

This movement will chart an enlightened and alternative path, providing information to families refusing to participate in globalist policies that disregard the traditional role of parents and guardians in nurturing and welfare of our children.

Climate Change

Evidence now proves that climate change is a massive, coordinated fraud, and the mainstream media deliberately lies to the public about climate change to push anti-free market schemes that would destroy the economy while transferring literally trillions of dollars into the pockets of wealthy globalists as part of a "carbon tax" transfer scheme.

Mankind's consumption of hydrocarbons is insignificant compared to the power of the sun and other cosmic influences. Research can confirm that all the hydrocarbons consumption in the world barely contributes anything to actual global temperatures. Carbon dioxide isn't the "pollutant" that climate change alarmists have long claimed. CO_2 won't destroy the planet and barely has any effect on global temperatures.

Carbon isn't the problem at all, in fact, carbon dioxide is re-greening the Earth on a massive scale by supporting the growth of rainforests, trees, and grasslands - Canada's vast forest cover is more than capable of absorbing the country's insignificant CO_2 emissions. Our local economies can only grow and prosper by opposing carbon taxation, which is significantly contributing to inflation to our detriment.

Independent candidates are free to expose the deliberate disinformation and focus on pragmatic solutions that balance environmental concerns with economic growth.

Individual Rights and Medical Freedom

Without repercussion, independent voices in government can promote the basic principles laid out in the Nuremberg Code and inform the public of the fundamental principles that have been violated by the authorities to advance their globalist agenda. Most importantly, it is our duty to uphold the fundamental principle of bodily autonomy. As we saw during the COVID debacle, no one should be forced to undergo a medical experiment without informed consent.

Despite the opposition from over 85,000 doctors, nurses, virologists, and epidemiologists, the experiment does not end. In fact, there are currently many attempts to change laws to enforce harmful vaccine compliance. Politicians, the media, and movie actors who claim that vaccines are safe and effective are not qualified to make such statements. They are simply paid propogandists, not independent medical scientists.

Independents are not constrained by party and political agendas that parrot the globalist privately financed health agendas as promoted by such non-elected organizations as the Bill and Melinda Gates Foundation, the World Health Organization (WHO), the Center for Disease Control (CDC), and the World Economic Forum (WEF).

We have an obligation to actively expose and hold accountable all levels of government and globalist entities that violate our fundamental medical right to make informed medical choices and will never again allow uninformed consent for experimental treatments on any individual.

People no longer want to be held hostage by top-down governance, where politicians only meaningfully interact with the public at election time. After the polls close, the winners break the promises that brought them to power and introduce all kinds of laws and mandates designed to control the public. The electorate currently feels powerless to stop these unsound and ineffective policies from being jammed down their throats.

Independent representatives will have a free vote on all new laws, not restricted to voting as they are told by the party whip and leader. They can table legislation that helps all of us without biased party approval. Working collaboratively with all other independent MLA's consensus can be reached focusing on what the voters actually want, not what a party leader or their puppet masters dictate.

In a political landscape dominated by party politics, the winds of change are building momentum. By running independent candidates in each of the provincial ridings, the broken and ineffective party system will be challenged and a new fresh approach based on the principles of truth, honesty, and integrity will be launched.

In this movements, independent representatives are advocates, voices, and allies responsible only to those they represent. Collectively, they can challenge the status quo and embark on a new path towards genuine representation, a stronger economy, and a brighter future for Nova Scotia - finally, a workable solution to the benefit of all.

Our goal to coalesce a bottom-up grassroots initiative across 55 Nova Scotia ridings as we spread the word about "A NEW WAY TO VOTE" will elect trusted persons in our communities to represent us as Independent MLAs in the NS Legislature.

Change will not happen without a fight. In Nova Scotia the law establishing a fixed election date implemented as a campaign promise by Premier Houston was then broken by the Premier by calling a snap election for 26 November 2024, eight months before his legislated mandate expired. This was done in large part because of the mobilization and candidate recruitment process of the growing independent movement. Furthermore, through the politically controlled NS Elections Commissions independent candidates have been blocked by rules and regulations designed to keep them of the ballot.

On behalf of the sovereign peoples of Nova Scotia who have been either directly or indirectly prevented from selecting an independent candidate to represent them in the legislature, the Independent NS Initiative Society along with the independent candidates whose chartered rights have been denied have called for a judicial review of the government's activities. The battle lines have been drawn.

There are those among us who have come to this planet as 'Way Showers' with a coded blueprint to carry light and to bring about a huge planetary transformation. Upon hearing the clarion call, the Way Showers will come out of the woodwork and be recognized as the Independent Candidates; the standard bearers that will lead the way and set the pace to freedom and autonomy in our public affairs.

A Journey of Discovery

This is not a book about government, it is a book about the personality traits and strengths that gave me the courage to do what I have come to do in this life by tapping into and using that inherent connection with spirit to guide me every step of the way. For more than forty years, my daily prayer to God upon awakening has been and continues to be.

Thank you for the returning consciousness and the opportunity of spending one more day in the fulfillment of Thy decrees. I humbly beseech my cosmic masters that I may be used as an instrument of service so that sincere seekers of the greater light may be shown the way by the light of my life this day. Keep me constantly attuned to Thy mind and Thy heart so that I may be more readily inspired. So-Mote-It-Be.

Although my views may seem out-of-step with society, that is okay. I have come to the understanding that although am living in this world I am not of this world and am part of a much larger multidimensional existence.

A synopsis of my personality characteristics gives me much to reflect upon and to work on to come to an understanding of how my soul is programmed to navigate the ups and downs, the triumphs, and disasters in the game of life. Through my life experiences I am confirming that there is no right or wrong path, that life is not inherently good or evil, it is all experience, and we must play the part that we have chosen prior to this incarnation. Acceptance of what is and dealing with what is in front of me through taking the positive path or choice at every turn is leading me slowly but surely to my destination of fulfilling the lesson plan of my life. At this point in time, I had much ahead of me to work on.

I do not like being pressured by others to conform to the programming of society and prefer to live in the present moment accepting and validating the legitimacy of the choices I make along with those made by others in each of their individual journeys. The motto "you do what you want, and I'll do what I want." resonates with me completely.

By going with the flow, I have learned not to resist life. By recognizing and accepting the things that cannot be changed without fanfare allows me to adapt to the many surprises in life that come my way. Materialistic pursuits are of little interest, and although I am often looked upon as eccentric, this aligns with another personal motto of mine ... "If the masses do it, don't!"

It is important for me to behave compassionately and helpfully in whatever situation or relationship I find myself in. My tendency is to look for a meeting of minds by pointing out the ways that things are similar, rather than the ways they are different. I try to avoid disagreements but won't back down from what is right. Relationships and compatibility along with finding common ground with others is most important. When dislike is expressed toward me, I am generally conciliatory without compromising my integrity. Where there is conflict, I will want to reconcile the differences and have the ability to find a larger perspective which encompasses alternative points of view. My tendency is to think well of others wishing only the best for them while working towards being loving, polite, cooperative, and tactful in all situations.

I am inclined to persevere and to keep going in spite of hardships and obstacles; doing something despite how hard it is or how long it takes to reach my goal. Being self-disciplined, setbacks that come my way are managed in stride. Once my routines are established, I will stick with them and can be counted on to endure with unwavering tenacity and steadfastness.

My preference is to live simply without adornment or embellishment. Because of my belief that nothing can truly upset me without my consent, trials and tribulations do not deter me. Known for being cool under pressure, I remain steadfast during times of stress while maintaining a serene disposition in the most chaotic situations deriving meaning from the acceptance of what life brings, with the self-discipline to endure all challenges with honor and good character. Living in the moment doing what is in front of me gives me a sense of satisfaction in everyday tasks knowing that there are no accidents because the world is unfolding exactly as it should. For me, it doesn't matter so much what's going on out there; what matters is that I stay in a state of serenity and accept the "isness" of life without judgement and that I am constantly attuned to the Divinity within.

I work on regulating my impatience, to overcome not wanting to wait and doing things before adequate preparations have been made. The career choice as an engineer involved with the planning and execution of major design and construction projects with multi disciplined teams and personalities was helped me work on this. As a soul learning to overcome impatience I am well served by reflecting on the proverb "haste makes waste". The primary lesson to be learned from impatience is to balance an overabundance of self-respect and to accept that all are equally worthy of the same respect. In life, there are neither winners nor losers, only players who are acting out a role; there is neither success nor failure, only experience; there is neither too much time nor too little, just enough to do what we have come to do.

To counteract impatience, I find it helpful to work on maintaining a sense of peace and tranquility at all times. It is one thing to be peaceful when everything is going my way and quite another when it is not. By pausing a moment and taking a conscious breath at the start of any exasperating situation and transforming the feelings that start to well up from within to that of peace, impatience can be mastered.

From the time as a young man, I believed I was special and destined for greatness. Those feelings come from an attitude of arrogance, and it was important in this lifetime to counteract this sense of superiority. Thinking that I was special and not subject to the same imperfections as others. I went through life with a feeling that all of the accolades and good fortune that came my way were well deserved and that good luck has nothing to do with it. My exaggerated sense of importance, perceiving myself beyond and above average, and capable of making a significant contribution to the world has led to profound lessons in humility.

As a soul who has lived many lives, I have come into this life to pass the test of the human journey to step over my disappointment in the world, my pain, my losses and to rise into my awareness that I am here to be loving, forgiving, compassionate and kind and ultimately that I am on the path of making a difference in the world.

In my career as an engineer and manager my primary focus was always to be considerate and empowering to others. However now I feel another calling to step up to a higher level of my soul wisdom with even more intention to helping others on a larger scale.

I have learned and am learning more everyday about quieting the mind and embracing my loving compassion and forgiveness for the world and realizing that it is more than just in the little things that I have done but now being called to a bigger expression of that helping work that will make a difference in the world. I feel now that I am being called to be the bridge to the invisible realm for others, to help uplift others to see and know that God consciousness is simply a loving force that rules the universe and that all of us are called at the end to be loving divine beings no matter how we may have behaved on our journeys. This calling is most aptly stated in the following message received from my spirit guides:

"Michael, you have served the human evolution well and learned the truth about your role as a teacher of higher understanding even as a business manager you have let kindness and compassion rule your choices which is excellent... well done. You are to take heart and lift into your spiritual wisdom as the teacher you have always been on earth to be, releasing your tight grip on the practical, the logical, and allowing your place as the healed and enlightened teacher to unfold boldly in the world. That's how you show up now, teach what you know is true and don't hold back. Shift from the left brain centered work and career to applying the higher spiritual wisdom that you have had coming into your heart for many decades on your lifetime journey. You have

had out-of-body experiences and spiritual experiences that have shown you for sure that the physical world is just an illusion. It is the time that you speak the truth of this and promote the wisdom of the soul's journey on earth and help others understand the consciousness of Divine love that rules the Universe."

END

Printed in the United States
by Baker & Taylor Publisher Services